The Wheel of Becoming

The Wheel of Becoming

•

Augustin Belisle

ST. BEDE'S PUBLICATIONS
Petersham, Massachusetts

Copyright © 1987 by Augustin Belisle, OSB
All Rights Reserved
PRINTED IN THE UNITED STATES OF AMERICA
4   3   2

Imprimatur: +Timothy J. Harrington
Bishop of Worcester
August 25, 1987

The *Imprimatur* is an official declaration that a book or pamphlet is considered to be free of doctrinal and moral error. It is not implied that those who have granted the *Imprimatur* necessarily agree with the contents, opinions, or statements expressed.

Acknowledgments

I wish to thank Bro. Aaron Jensen, OSB, for the many hours of proofreading which he accorded this book. Also, I am indebted to Fr. Gerard Kirsch, OSB, for his encouragement and insight.

Scripture texts used in this work are taken from the *New American Bible*, copyright © 1970, by the Confraternity of Christian Doctrine, Washington, D.C. Used by permission of the copyright owner. All rights reserved.

Liturgical texts used in this work are from the English translation of *The Roman Missal* copyright © 1973, International Committee on English in the Liturgy, Inc. All rights reserved. Used with permission.

Cover design by Basil J. Atwell, OSB

LIBRARY OF CONGRESS CATALOGING IN PUBLICATION DATA

Belisle, Augustin, 1947-
  The Wheel of becoming.

  1. Spiritual life—Catholic authors.   2. Church year.   I. Title.
BX2350.2.B4215   1987   242'.3   87-26493
ISBN 0-932506-57-7

Published by St. Bede's Publications
      P.O. Box 545
      Petersham, MA 01366-0545

To my brothers in community—
the monks of Assumption Abbey

Contents

	Introduction — The Wheel of Becoming	ix
I	A Time for Watching — ADVENT	3
II	A Time for Birthing — CHRISTMAS/EPIPHANY	12
III	A Time for Giving — LENT	23
IV	A Time for Dying — HOLY WEEK	36
V	A Time for Rising — EASTER	47
VI	A Time for Believing — ASCENSION/PENTECOST	59
VII	A Time for Living — ORDINARY TIME	71
VIII	The Inspirable Life	84

Introduction
The Wheel of Becoming

There is something rather attractive about things which move in circles. Whether they are picturesque windmills, the pirouetting skates of an ice dancer, satellites revolving in superterrestrial orbit, or Tibetan Buddhist prayer wheels churning out petitions to the cosmos, objects which move around and around in successive circular paths fascinate us.

The attention we pay to round things comes naturally enough. We are surrounded by circles and spheres, discs, balls, and cylinders. Time's measurement, as well as our personal and collective passages through time's rituals, follow this same circular movement in set circuits and established cycles. We count off chronological time in spaced circuits of minutes, hours, days, weeks, months, years, decades, centuries. Even the archaeologists and geophysicists, who have the earth's calendar nicely layered in linear strata covering millions and billions of years, are basing their measurements on the cyclical orbits of our planet around its star. And everything we know empirically is, in some sense, moving around in roughly circular motion.

The circle is representative of infinity because it has no boundaries or defined limits. Circles have no beginning and no end. The movement of circular form is endless movement, perpetual motion. This ceaseless movement around a path without end beckons us to infinite mystery which lies above and beyond us. The circle can call the human heart to mystery.

But the circle calls humanity to meaning as well as to mystery. In an archetypal and universal way, this symbol evokes within us the search for ultimate meaning. Transcending the limits of time and space by which we sense ourselves as bound to this empirical human existence, the symbol of roundness calls us to eternity (the timeless) and to infinity (the spaceless). The circle signifies the timeless quality of ultimate meaning for a humanity stretching its arms in a reach beyond the stars and probing with its ears a silence within the atom.

The entire life span of a human being forms a delicate counterpoint to these melodies of mystery and meaning. From the stage of infancy to the experience of old age, the harmony resulting from any individual's play at this counterpoint will be a unique personal response to what is perceived and experienced as infinite and eternal.

When circular forms are placed one within another, concentrically, the movement envisioned is both the inward movement toward the inner circle's core and also the outward movement from the core to the outer circles. Students of religion have seen in the concentric circles' outward movement a call to the infinite, a desire for transcendence. Correspondingly, the inward motion of concentric circles symbolically expresses immanence. I think that is why Pierre Teilhard de Chardin used the image of a cone spiralling into the universe when describing what he meant by the convergence of all spiritual energies into the universal presence of a Cosmic Christ. Teilhard de Chardin took care to have his readers understand that the spiralling energy was not in the shape of a coil composed of similarly proportioned circles. The spiral is a cone with ever decreasing circles moving upward and inward. The effect for the poetically sensitive reader is, again, a desire for transcendence and an expression of immanence—the power and presence of God in a universe which groans under the labors of bringing Christ to birth on a cosmic scale.

The real point of interest in the circle, sphere, and wheel is the focal point—the center. In this center one can find the source of energy which causes the movement of the circle. In the center one can discover cosmic energy. This inner core as focal point becomes the center of the world, the core of the universe which both concentrates and radiates motion. The central focus draws us toward, and emanates power from, itself. It is mystery and revelation. We are drawn to the center, any center. We like to get at the core of something. Within the center is the metaphysical core, the essence of being. As we become united with this focal point, we are enabled to become who we are in relationship to the cosmos—one with the universe.

From the perspectives of different disciplines, many authors have written that the process of centering is psychologically and spiritually (if not physiologically) integral to the formation of human personality. Is it not intrinsic to human nature for a person to gravitate toward the center of her or his own being, where true humanity in relation to the sacred realities can be found? A Christian mystic might say that the living waters to which Jesus referred in his dialogue with the Samaritan woman at the well flow at this center. Here the ineffable mystery of life can be articulated without words. Here the tiny whispering sound in the wind can be heard. At the metaphysical center one is drawn to become what one is. The reality of the center is the reality of now. When we find ourselves at the center, we discover the potential which is always present. The center has no beginning or end, it simply *is*. And it *is* over and over again in the eternal present of time in relation to God. If we are faithful to the centering process and open to its revelations, we catch glimpses and experience nuances of a deeper and more consummate life than that empirical existence which we presume to be so real and so apical.

As we attempt our various processes of centering throughout our time together on earth, our circles become cycles. We construct various cycles in our lives, mirroring other cycles we see in the world and the universe around us. From individuals, families and communities, to nations and peoples—everyone follows rituals.

Ritual in the religious sphere is embodied in well-defined cycles of time and tradition. The various cycles of the Church Year are designed to give us, as much as possible, the whole picture of salvation history and celebration for a pilgrim people on their way to the Parousia.

The development of the Church's liturgical year was a long and complicated, though admittedly quite fascinating, process. It is not my intention to reflect on the ins and outs of this historical process. Many fine studies of liturgical history by competent and articulate scholars are readily available. Religious bookstores are also well stocked with volumes of commentaries on the scriptural texts used throughout the liturgical seasons. My intention for this book is to reflect on the seasonal cycle of the liturgical year, centering on the presence of Christ and the seasonal spiritual signs which are inherent for us throughout the cycle.

The liturgical seasons celebrate the various mysteries of Christ whose paschal presence is always at the center of the cycle. The paschal mystery permeates all celebrations, all liturgies and all seasons with its central significance. Since Jesus is our model who has shown us the way to God, we consider Christ to be the fullest expression of what it means to be human. Jesus is our paradigm of human life at the center. Our celebrations of Christ throughout the year are really celebrations of human life at its fullest, throughout the various seasons of the year. We discern our human cycles within the liturgical year's cycle of Christ's words, deeds, and experiences.

With the cycle of liturgical seasons, we celebrate the

greatest circle in our lives. Year after year we pass through the various mysteries contained in the paschal mystery. We follow the changing seasons with our cyclical calendar. The turning cycle is a great wheel of becoming for those who discern the presence of human becoming inherent in it. In its revolutions we can find the fullness for which we search, yet already possess in the presence of the Risen Christ. At its center we can embrace our own wholeness in the living Christ whose presence we encounter in every liturgy we celebrate. Like other significant circles, the liturgical cycle draws us to the sacred, speaking a word of infinity and eternity. As we celebrate our annual repetition of the events surrounding the life, death, and resurrection of Jesus Christ—as our wheel of becoming turns each year—we touch upon essential and ultimate meaning.

What I hope to accomplish in this reflective book is to indicate how, in our cyclical ordering and repetitive cultic centering, the liturgical cycle of seasons taps the very ground of our existence as human persons. The liturgical seasons are our taproots, as it were. The Paschal Mystery of Christ has everything to say to us about becoming human. All the rhythms of life are present in the liturgical year. Our own becoming within the framework of the liturgy is but a cycle within the greater cycle, if we are open to the cycle's turning. If our life-rhythms mirror the paschal rhythms of new life in Christ, then we ourselves are wheels of becoming. Then we are wheels within the wheel. And the center is quiet communion.

The Wheel of Becoming

I
A Time for Watching — ADVENT

Autumn has thrown down summer's gauntlet, soon to be snatched up by the gelid fingers of winter's enduring grasp on Dakota prairies. The passing days of vibrant autumnal colors exude the unique excitement of the Fall season—a fascination with piquant pleasures for the eyes and nose of one who notices the vigorous display of nature's passage from blossoming and fruition to watching and waiting.

For those of us who enjoy the full circle of nature's four seasons, autumn carries us quite naturally into the liturgical celebration of Advent. Grey forlorn trees, stripped of their foliage, remind us of the essentially ephemeral quality of human existence, as well as of the cycles of ongoing birth, death, and rebirth throughout the splendid panoply of natural and cosmic cycles around us—and within us. The shriveled remains of frostbitten flowering plants remind us of some of the joy of what has been. Like ourselves, they return to a receptive cycle of awaiting right conditions. In their dormancy, they call our minds to the budding time still to come.

The cold, blustery winds of November and December can chill us to the bone, but these same currents are fragrant with freshness and the promise of something new. Within the scent of plant decay and frozen earth lies the tantalizing aroma of next year's seed breaking into bloom and next spring's soil teeming with a wondrously diverse abundance of animated stir. We anticipate next year's bouquet in the sweet-sour perfume of this year's withering.

Our skies are filled with the huge cumulus clouds of what one of my confreres calls "those wonderful Romanesque days" of autumn on the prairies. The clouds of autumn are puffing and piling masses, ponderous and somewhat obstructive to the view. But in their rapidly changing motion, these same clouds are revelatory to the eye which can detect within their modulations the postludes of past recollection and the preludes of future portent. At times the clouds of Fall bring early snows, precursors of bleak wintry nights of vigilance and expectation.

The season of autumn lends itself to the concurrent Christian experience of the Advent season. Within the circular rhythm of the liturgical year, our human rhythm becomes a time for waiting and watching.

Waiting is a disposition and action with which we are all familiar. In a sense, every passing instant of time is a moment of waiting—a passage of leaving off from what has been to an assuming of what is yet to be. In this passing from past to future, we wait in the present. And there are so many aspects to our present waiting, so many waitings. Waiting tries somehow to put time in suspension, playing upon the theme of future possibility. Variations on this theme color the contours of human personality.

There are different kinds of waiting: active and passive ways to wait, helpful and hindering, open and closed, purposeful and aimless, aware and oblivious, authentic and disingenuous. One of the deadliest kinds of waiting is waiting by the clock. Clock-time waiting can numb one against the ongoing rhythms of life within and around oneself by concentrating attention and energy on the ticking time clock which never quite manages to tick fast enough! One can forget that the time clock on the wall is only a mechanism for the measurement of chronological time, not a regulator for the ebb and flow of the human tides of personhood.

How we wait is vitally important to our spiritual maturity, as well as to our psychological growth. Within a Christian context, waiting should be time spent at the center of things. Being at the center is the type of waiting fostered by the season of Advent.

Many different waitings await us all on our Advent journey through the cycles of birth and death. The Church season of Advent gives us glimpses of *how* we should wait by celebrations of both these aspects of one same reality. We are born that we might die, and we die that we might truly live. But so much of our living and dying is contained in the waiting.

Christian waiting is not aimless waiting, but a watching in expectation of all God's comings into our world. Hopeful watching becomes the primary spiritual sign of the Advent liturgical cycle. The long four-week vigil is kept in anticipation of the Church's annual celebration of the historical event of God's Incarnation in the person of Jesus of Nazareth. While we prepare for the celebration of incarnational mystery, we remind ourselves of another advent still to occur—the second coming of a glorified and universal Christ in the eschatological power of fulfillment. Within the image of swaddling clothes in an animals' feeding trough lies the likeness of Parousia. And the vigilance of human expectancy discovers both fullness and foreshadowing in a baby's birth. For incarnation is past event, present reality and future hope. The rhythms of human vigilance watch, as it were, these three dimensions coalescing into the very core of all we know and for which we hope.

When we keep vigil, we are watching and waiting for someone or something with which we are, directly or indirectly, familiar. Advent vigilance is watching for someone we love—an experience we all know well, a cycle we enter repeatedly during our lives of relatedness. It is quite human to be aware of the future, to be expectant upon the people, places, and events which may either directly effect or tangentially affect what the morrow might hold for us. When we are watching for a loved one, our vigilance assumes a certain air of intensity which can transform its future resolution into an event of moment.

This is not overstressing the importance of human watching and waiting. The existential act of watching, in expectation of whatever happening, pulls us into the human cycles of contingency. We watch and wait upon the future, just as countless generations of vigilant women and men have done in the past. How many ages of humanity's history passed in search of meaning within redemption before Jesus of Nazareth's coming responded to those ages of vigilance! How long will we celebrate the present comings of Christ into our lives and expectantly watch for that future advent in fullness and finality? We do not know the duration of our vigilance, but the annual Advent cycle stresses that watchfulness is an important part of what it means to be human. Within each year's turning, we spend some four weeks of "the watchful night" to call ourselves to the rhythms of incarnation and redemption. Our watchful night looks to the Second Epistle of Peter for inspiration: "Keep your attention closely fixed on it, as you would on a lamp shining in a dark place until the first streaks of dawn appear and the morning star rises in your hearts" (2 Pt. 1:19).

One of the ascetical practices among early Christian believers was to keep a watchful night by going without sleep and spending the time in prayer. Various monastic groups today mirror this Christian asceticism by celebrating an Office of Vigils during the pre-dawn hours. Monks and nuns serve as signs of humanity's waiting and watching by becoming living Christian symbols of the praying Church, watching for the imminent dawning of the Parousia upon the shadows of a world in flux. The Advent season accords the universal Church the opportunity to keep vigil in a concerted way and to live liturgically that symbol of Christian watchfulness.

> In his love Christ has filled us with joy
> as we prepare to celebrate his birth,
> so that when he comes he may find us watching in prayer,
> our hearts filled with wonder and praise (Advent Preface 2).

Christian vigilance is not a passive regard for whatever might happen in the course of destiny. The human cycle embodied by the Advent season is an active search, enlivened by hope. The Christian faith never yields to the pessimism which despises humanity or despairs of divinity. The expectancy of Advent emphasizes the necessity for hope. Each Christian furthers the development of his or her own personhood by becoming a sign of hope in the world. The destructive circles of despair which seemingly pervade the global affairs of humanity can be transformed into nuturing cycles of hope by the centering process of awareness which discerns God's comings within humanity's goings.

Hopefulness heightens our sensitivity to spiritual realities. Hope sharpens our awareness, enabling us to recognize better God's presence in our lives. If we find ourselves without hope—if we are, in fact, hopeless—we are already predisposed to ignore the epiphanies of God's advent into the limited world of our own comings and goings. Hope expands where despair curtails and constricts. The hopefulness of Advent expectation expands the limits of our powers to perceive and recognize. Hopeful watching is also a source of joy for the watcher and the entire Christian community. The deep inner joy of hopeful vigilance stems from the essential paradox of Christian life: we watch and wait for what we already know and possess, although not fully. And our joy is expressed in the gratitude, reconciliation and peace we know in our experience and celebration of the living presence of Christ in the Eucharist.

The Advent expectancy which Christians live throughout the broad expanse stretching from Jesus' historical birth in Bethlehem of Judea to the future coming of Christ at the end of time is a vigilance sustained by eucharistic gratitude. The very meaning of "eucharist" is gratitude, and the joy which believers experience in the presence of the Eucharist is a deep thanksgiving for the gift of shared life and love. Sharing eucharist is another way of being at the center; it reconciles disparate parts and heals the ruptures of human existence. Eucharistic reconciliation demands, in virtue of authentic witness, that we all really be reconciled with one another. We are asked to be bread for one another in eucharistic expectation. Becoming eucharist for each other incarnates the hope for peace in this world.

Those who are watching for the advent of God express their hopeful vigilance in peacemaking. How could the Advent cycle of human vigilance be otherwise? In spite of ourselves, we are prodded to peace by the Gospel goad which delineates our path between Christ's two comings. This peacemaking born of hope underpins the entire Gospel journey between these two advents and achieves its goal if we are at peace both within ourselves and with one another. Both dynamics of peacemaking bring true hope to a watching, waiting world. Here hope for a genuinely renewed humanity can find space and take root in the ground of graceful readiness.

Every human life has its own relationship with the sacred. Each person knows his or her own inner world of spiritual realities where he or she can become aware of God's presence in the midst of all the tugs and pulls of human personality. With the world's present complexities demanding of us so much precious personal energy in order to cope with so-called "reality," it might be considered a minor miracle whenever someone actually recognizes God's present comings into our world! But God's advent into the thoughts, feelings, and actions of human lives and affairs really is an everyday event. Our contemporary human challenge is to stay awake to that divine presence which warms the hearts, enlightens the minds, and quickens the bodies of those who are not too impetuous to wait nor too dispirited to watch. Each coming of Christ in the power of God's Spirit is a further elaboration of God's ever-unfolding self-revelation.

Revelation is a process in which each moment of God's coming into the world is a new beginning. The unfurling epiphanies of God's presence are always at hand for the heart that waits and the soul that watches. Setting our hearts on the unveiling of revelation is like peeling an onion. Each layer tearfully uncovers another layer, until the core is laid bare as a quiet, tearless stillness at the center. With our acceptance of a paradoxical life in the presence of Christ, our joy is at that center. This joy is a messianic joy which remembers a birth some two thousand years ago in a small town in Asia's Middle East and savors each and every rebirth of messianic presence in the Spirited existence we call "Church."

Advent also watches for the future coming of the glorified Christ, but stresses that this future coming is the coming of *our* future. We expect to find ourselves at last in the Cosmic Christ, who will be the ultimate resolution of our long wait and the light which will dawn on the enduring vigil kept by humanity. Christian watching is a careful and enlivened waiting upon the presence of the Lord until all is brought to fulfillment in that presence.

Advent vigilance consciously accents humanity's emptiness in light of that future vision of fullness and fulfillment. The three cycles of Advent's liturgical readings sound forth calls for preparation and readiness for all the comings of Christ into our world. As we prepare ourselves to celebrate incarnational mystery, we embrace our own emptiness. As we call ourselves to a constant readiness for Christ's Second Coming, we yearn for our own fulfillment which can only be found in God's fullness.

Like the prophets before him in the history of Israel's salvation, Jesus Christ spoke of the "great day." Prophets have referred to the eschaton—the end of time—as "that day," the "day of the Lord," "that great and terrible day," the "day of judgment," that "day of days." In the Lucan account of the Parousia (Lk. 21:25-36), Jesus gave a verbal depiction of the end of time, using the eschatological signs and images of his time and culture—replete with death, anguish, fear, upheaval, celestial disturbances, and the Son of Man enthroned on a cloud.

But Christ told his disciples that they could and should prepare for that day by avoiding self-indulgence and self-centered existence. Jesus used the images of being bloated with indulgence, drunk, and caught up in worldly cares. Disciples would have to be on their guard and vigilant, pray constantly and stand secure against the encroachments of self on God's presence. Otherwise, the end would close in on them like a trap. They would become ensnared by their own lack of attention, their carelessness and self-orientation.

But in the midst of all the apocalyptic chaos, Jesus gave words of hopeful expectancy to humanity: "When these things begin to happen, stand erect and hold your heads high, for your deliverance is near at hand" (Lk. 21:28). This is the posture of resurrection—standing with heads raised. Watchfulness and prayer will prepare the disciples for the eschaton, so they can truly stand secure.

How can we prepare for Christ's coming in glory? How do we meet Christ in Advent? How should we meet the Lord in any of his comings? Jesus cautioned us to be awake, watching, and prayerful. In hopeful expectation, we are still waiting for the Lord and watching for his advent. Our prayer for one another should be the desire Paul expressed for the Christian community at Thessalonica: "And may the Lord increase you and make you overflow with love for one another and for all, even as our love does for you. May he strengthen your hearts, making them blameless and holy before our God and Father at the coming of our Lord Jesus with all his holy ones" (1 Thess. 3:12-13). Our Advent cycle of watching is founded on hope; our hope is grounded in love. Between this founding and grounding lies the pure gift of faith, the bonding of our Christian life together.

The world is being divinized by our participation in divine life around and within ourselves. To the extent that we recognize this sacred presence and allow it to permeate what we do and who we become, we bridge the seeming chasm between the past and future advents of Christ. All God's present comings advance a gentle perception which encircles the cosmos, penetrating the ages of humanity's obduracy, and draws our hearts toward the center as a wheel's spokes refer to the hub. And we are most aware of that animated core in our very human cycles of waiting and watching.

II
A Time for Birthing —
CHRISTMAS/EPIPHANY

Those of us who, by choice or by chance, style ourselves "northerners," feel the impact of what winter can hold for human beings more directly than those who live in more temperate climes. The northern Plains States experience most consistently the harsh weather conditions which the winter season can offer those of us who undergo this annual experience of starkness, austerity, and restlessness. Prairie people suffer a long winter, knowing what it is to wait out a blizzard and to prepare for the long freeze.

Yet there is a certain compelling, even riveting quality experienced when walking over prairie fields or through the trees of deep coulees blanketed with snow. The stark simplicity of the landscape arrests our own movement as it transforms the rustle and flurry of autumn into the quiet stillness of winter. Even when wintry winds wend their way through barren branches with the *woosh* which seems to break the calm called for by December snows, our hearts are nevertheless quieted by the stark reality paradoxically exposed by winter's cover.

I suspect that most of us longingly wait for the end of winter before it has even begun its assault on our senses, but, personally, I look forward to winter's onset, just as I anticipate each season in its turn of the cycle. However, I can understand how the restrictions of movement and the limited options which wintry conditions place upon us force us into a mode of introspection, the duration of which can easily prove stressful for unwilling participants. The psychology of receptiveness which winter forces upon our active bodies and restless minds well suits both the Advent and Christmas seasons which occur during this time of waiting, inner discovery, and temporal stillness.

Winter's austerity can be severe and forbidding. Within its harshness we call to mind our own fragility and emptiness. I am drawn to rivers during the winter season when the surface is frozen, wearing a light dusting of morning snow. I know that water flows beneath it all, but I hear nothing of its currents in the crisp, silent air. When I am near a river, iced over and silently winding through winter's pale trees, I feel fragile and alone. But the aloneness is a comforting solitude, not the desolate loneliness of a human person without the blessings of full communion with God. And just as spring follows winter in the ongoing cycle of seasonal change, we know through religious experience and by spiritual intuition that Christmas follows Advent—our personal emptiness will be filled with God's presence; our expectant waiting will reach fulfillment.

As we peer at an austere landscape through a frosted pane, we not only know the warmth of present waiting, but also the hope and adventure of future promise. Our wintering hearts look within the crystalized wonder of frost forming on the windowlight and recognize, with gratitude, the presence of God's Word welling within, waiting to be born again and again. The Word of God is restless, as it were, urging us to bring it to full term and fruition.

We can reflect this restlessness to be born by our own anxieties about spiritual birthing. Just as we can find ourselves fidgety during winter months with an uneasy "cabin fever," Advent accentuates a certain unrest we experience —the desire to celebrate the Christmas Mystery of the Incarnation and to incarnate, in our own sacramental lives, the presence of God's Word among us.

Those of us who are fortunate enough to enjoy nature's

canopy through a relatively unpolluted atmosphere, can be mesmerized by endless layers of celestial bodies glistening in the skies of a winter's night. When a crisp, frosty night with a cloudless sky is matched with the fluffy dusting of a dry snow, the sparkling effect of both earth and sky can be dazzling and wondrous. We can be swept out of ourselves by the splendor of it all. In their own way, our seasonal Christmas decorations are designed for just such sweeping experiences. All the colored lights and the ornaments which reflect their glow, take us into a mythical realm of childhood regained, while highlighting the festivities surrounding the celebration of Jesus' birth in history. Light bulbs adorn our home exteriors, festive trees and fireplaces, our commercial buildings and streets, even our churches. By means of their luminosity, we awaken ourselves to the end of the Advent cycle of waiting and the commencement of the Christmas and Epiphany cycles of fulfillment. Now the long-awaited Word is spoken; the promise is fulfilled.

The annual repetition of the Christmas and Epiphany cycles celebrates our human cycles of renewal as incarnational light dawns in our hearts. Light symbolism has consistently spoken to human religious consciousness of life, creation, sustenance, and fertility. Many religious traditions contain myths of origin which explain human existence in reference to the sun. For example, Inca myths refer to humanity as "children of the sun." Within the Christian tradition, Christ's presence is often expressed in terms of light imagery, especially in connection with the mysteries of Incarnation and Resurrection. In the Christmas and Epiphany celebrations, Jesus Christ becomes: "the dawn of salvation," "the new light," "rising dawn," "true light of the world," "the light of all nations," "bright dawn of your Word made flesh," and "the new and radiant vision of your glory." We ourselves become the "people of this light" who, in the cycles of our own human becoming, continue to follow the star of Incarnation Mystery and witness salvation's inbreaking.

Light played a significant role in the formation of the Church's historical celebration of Jesus' birth. Twice a year, the sun reaches its greatest declination from the equator, north or south. At these times, the sun seems to stand still for a few days, and we call this phenomenon "solstice," derived from the Latin words meaning "sun-standing-still." On our Gregorian calendar, the summer and winter solstices occur on June 21 and December 21, respectively. Evidently, the Emperor Aurelian proclaimed the Syrian sun-god Emesa as the chief patron of the Roman Empire on December 25, 274—the date for the winter solstice on the Julian calendar (January 6 on the Egyptian calendar). This annual commemoration, *Dies Natalis Solis Invicti* (Birthday of the Unconquered Sun), was to be celebrated every December 25. Due to recent historical research, and because patristic sources used the title "Sun of Justice" in reference to Jesus Christ, some scholars conjecture that the solstitial celebration of Christ's birth on December 25 in the Western Church was likely designed to counteract the influence of Emesa's solar devotees. Although the theory has not been proven conclusively, it does seem quite plausible.

The Eastern Church, however, celebrated the event on January 6 rather than December 25. The December Christmas feast seems to have spread to the East, as the January Epiphany feast spread to the West. The chief factor underpinning the Eastern adoption of the December date seems to have been the Arian denial of Christ's divinity rather than the cultic worship of the sun. To affirm that Christ was divine and to celebrate this Incarnation Mystery assumed dogmatic importance. Not surprisingly, the chief proponents of the December celebration in the Eastern Church were the leading anti-Arian Fathers of the Church: the Cappadocians Basil, Gregory of Nyssa and Gregory

Nazianzus, as well as John Chrysostom, Paul of Emesa, Ephrem, and others. Gradually, the Eastern Churches adopted the West's solstice date for the celebration of Christ's birth, not only as a memorial of the historical event, but also as a mystery feast of Incarnation similar to the mystery feast of Easter.

Just as the December solstice marks the lengthening of light after the period of darkness, Christmas and Epiphany celebrate the light dawning in our lives, in response to our human cycles of watching and waiting. The revolutions of our own passings from possibility to reality, darkness to light, emptiness to fullness, and from expectancy to giving birth, find archetypal significance within the turning wheel of liturgical observance. All these passings are paschal, just as all paschal realities are transitional and transformational. Within the birth of Jesus and the epiphanies of his divine life, we discover our own lives' meaning and a pattern for the articulation of that meaning as a way to share in that divine life.

What is this incarnational light which illumines our days until the consummation of time, the finale of humanity's movement toward the center? The great joy of Christian faith is derived from the truth that this "what" is a "who"—Jesus Christ's living presence among us! The theme of Incarnation plays upon the heartstrings of our lives with inexorable exigency and through an endless stream of variations. Our Christmas light is like the reassuring lambency of logs in a wilderness campfire. We have journeyed together on the trek of human becoming; the trekking has been arduous and, at times, hazardous. In the warmth of the fire we seek protection from the cold phantoms of fear, and security from the dark shadows of uncertainty. We are drawn to the light of Christmas, where we can experience the fellowship of God's People centering on the mystery of God becoming human, so that humanity might begin its journey into divine life. Incarnational light is paradoxical. The presence of Christ in humanity's history shows us that the only way to become truly human within an incarnational context is to share *divine* life and love. Our humanity is not annihilated in the dawn of salvation. Rather, in this light we find ourselves as we are meant to be.

Probably the most significant aspect of the Christmas liturgical cycle is that of fulfillment: Jesus of Nazareth becomes the fulfillment of salvation history's waiting for a promised redemption. Jesus is a model for us, the fullest expression of what it means to be a human person. Jesus Christ is the fulfillment of God's divine economy yet to be realized at the end of time. The Christmas Mystery, then, celebrates a triple mystery of comings: Jesus the Promised One, the Messiah, came into our human history, proclaimed the Good News of salvation, suffered death by crucifixion and resurrected from the dead; Jesus the Risen Lord presently comes into our lives in the power of the Holy Spirit; Jesus the Glorified One will come again at the eschaton. Each liturgical event of the Christmas cycle celebrates all three of these comings of Jesus into our lives: the historical past in Jesus of Nazareth, the existential present in the experience of the living presence of the Risen Lord, and the anticipated future of the Cosmic Christ toward whom all creation is converging.

Through the Incarnational Mystery, God's Word is most eloquently spoken to humanity which has waited in hopeful expectation for fulfillment. Jesus is the fulfillment of God's promised salvation. Jesus Christ is the Word spoken in all aspects of the divine liturgy in praise of God. In faith we listen to this Word given birth within ourselves, the power of God's Word coming into our hearts. In this Word we receive forgiveness, spiritual freedom, and the gift of eternal life. The Christmas and Epiphany cycles celebrate the presence of this fulfilling Word. Jesus is the Eternal Word, the future fulfillment already present in us. All the collected moments of human waiting and expectation have been gathered into a profound event which places us more efficaciously in God's presence, enablng us to participate in divine life. Christ is our fullness and, in that fullness, we are now a new creation.

When we embrace the Paschal Mystery in our lives now fulfilled by Jesus' self-gift, we come to know our own emptiness as the way to fullness. Within the depths of self-surrender, we come to the still center of Christ's all-encompassing love, and discover a fuller and truer self. This is the mystery of our fulfillment, our very divinization. Jesus Christ shines in the hearts of the new creation. And we respond to incarnational presence by nurturing the growth of the Word in our world and, in whatever possible ways, by giving birth to Christ through the flesh-and-blood ethics of Gospel love.

Already in our celebrations of the Christmas and Epiphany cycles, as well as any other liturgical season or celebration for that matter, we are deeply aware that the Word is a paschal Word. The Paschal Mystery is of central significance to the Church Year's entirety, and the birth of Jesus Christ is intimately linked with our salvation, oriented toward the Paschal Mystery, and only to be fully realized in the Parousia. Christmas is the birth of Easter. Epiphany is the manifestation of the Crucified Lord, lying in a manger. This is not a morbid downplay of incarnational joy; Christmas joy is a paschal joy which recognizes our human transition from death to life in the beginning of Jesus' transitions from life to death to new life.

Within the scope of each liturgical cycle, we celebrate all the mysteries of Christ in their entirety. These mysteries cannot be separated from one another. We recognize the Risen Lord in Bethlehem of Judea. We celebrate death on the Hill of Skulls already in the adoration of a baby by wise men from the East. The Christmas and Epiphany celebrations put us in contact with the mystery of salvation, prepare us better to understand Easter, and help us to live this Paschal Mystery efficaciously for others. If we do not celebrate all the present comings of Christ into our lives, how can we expect to recognize Christ in our future? Our incarnational witness will ground us in the great Easter Mystery of our redemption. All the liturgical seasons of the Church's turning wheel are bathed in this Easter light.

In the circumstances surrounding the event of Jesus' birth and the worship rendered him by the wise ones from the East, we recognize a great epiphany of God. Jesus Christ is manifested as Son of God and King. What we continue to perceive in the Incarnation Mystery throughout the centuries of post-resurrectional time is the loving presence of God. What we experience as this epiphany's challenge is the call to manifest Christ's presence for others. We are challenged to recognize the Incarnate Word in our midst, to worship Christ in honest humility and free detachment, and to manifest for others the presence whose life we celebrate. The Infancy Narrative of Saint Matthew's Gospel records that sages from the East prostrated themselves before the newborn child in Bethlehem. The light which draws into Christ's presence is a ray which penetrates the deepest recesses of ignorance and sinfulness, the hidden corners of egoism, and the thick walls of fear and hatred. We respond to this incarnational light as the Magi responded to a star. As they once offered their treasures to a king, we now offer the gift of ourselves to love's service.

We live during the ongoing manifestation of God's presence in the world. Every sacrament is an epiphany, and life in the Church of Christ (which is *the* sacrament) is the manifestation of Christ in all his mysteries. Christian life, too, is an epiphany, as we walk in the light of the Incarnate Word and Risen Lord—an epiphanic light whose rays illumine our ecclesial path. When we liturgically celebrate the memorial of the wise men lying prostrate before a baby in an animals' feeding trough, we enter the mystery of the eschatological Kingdom. Whereas they were enlightened by the compelling force of truth in the form of a star, that wisdom with which we ourselves might be blessed is kindled by the light of the Risen Christ—a light which has irrevocably altered the meaning of life.

We say that Jesus Christ is our paradigm, the model for becoming the fullest expression of what it means to be a human person.

> One of the scribes came up, and when he heard them arguing he realized how skillfully Jesus answered them. He decided to ask him, "Which is the first of all the commandments?" Jesus replied: "This is the first:
> 'Hear, O Israel! The Lord our God is Lord alone!
> Therefore you shall love the Lord your God
> with all your heart,
> with all your soul,
> with all your mind,
> and with all your strength.'
> This is the second,
> 'You shall love your neighbor as yourself.' There is no other commandment greater than these." The scribe said to him: "Excellent, Teacher! You are right in saying, 'He is the One, there is no other than he.' Yes, 'to love him with all our heart, with all our thoughts and with all our strength, and to love our neighbor as ourselves' is worth more than any burnt offering or sacrifice." Jesus approved the insight of this answer and told him, "You are not far from the reign of God" (Mk. 12:28-34).

The world's lovers are not far from God's Kingdom. Those who know how to love, freely and unreservedly, are close to God. Jesus Christ is our model for loving. We remember how he came to save us out of love, how he loved God and devoted himself to discerning and accomplishing God's will. We read his Gospel message of life and love. We recall how he touched the lives of those around him with compassion, understanding, and healing. We know that he loved those unloved by society—the social and religious outcasts, the diseased, public sinners, the poor, and oppressed. We celebrate our salvation because his immense capacity for loving led him to rejection, death, and new life.

If we see, hear, and feel Christ loving in the world, we know that God's Kingdom is proclaimed by the very act of loving. Love brings about the Kingdom. When the community called Church is truly the Body of Christ, it embodies God's reign. We give form to Christ in the world. If we are actually becoming Christ, then we are living as he lived. We are loving God and seeking God's will. We are loving those around us, thereby living our human personhood to the full. We reach out compassionately, caring for others' needs and sharing the grace we live. We love those unloved and forgotten, the misunderstood, and alienated. We embrace Christ throughout our cycles of birth and death. We give Christ flesh and blood in the world because he is present among us and within us. Becoming a person involves taking risks within the circles of love. The more genuine these circles are, the more inclusive and compenetrating they become. The circles of love gentle the cycles of life.

Our Christian way to deepen the efficacy of God's Kingdom is an incarnational path. We are born to a life which shows its most profound vitality in the act of giving birth. As the mystery of human existence takes on an animated portentousness in the process of physiological birth, the meaning of eternal life assumes greater significance each time we spiritually give birth to God's Word in the world. Being incarnational colors the landscape of love with many different hues. We enflesh the presence of the Word through our cycles of spiritual birthings. In faith we embrace the Word; by commitment, we proclaim what we have embraced. In prayer we awaken ourselves to the Word, listen to it, and nurture its growth. Through sacramental living we celebrate the Word's presence and share its essence with others. Acts of love give expression to the Word in the most incarnational ways of all.

The challenge of the Christmas Mystery with its mandate of epiphanic birthings of the Word is that we must take seriously the prospect of sharing the responsibility for a redeemed humanity's awareness of God's loving presence. Living incarnationally—giving birth to God's Word—enables us to taste the spirit of eternal life and to savor the tastings. We believe that Jesus came among us as a human person and that Christ comes among us still. The Christmas/Epiphany cycle of our Church celebration is a love cycle in which we recognize the great gift of God's love for us. With the Holy Week cycle, we will recognize the great depth of Christ's love for God and us. This is love which lasts, since Jesus Christ *is* love.

> We have seen his glory:
> The glory of an only Son coming from the Father,
> filled with enduring love (Jn 1·14)

The liturgical wheel keeps turning because this love perdures. Within that sacramental turning, the wheels of our own humanization turn only to the extent that we dare to love—hastening the world's divinization.

III
A Time for Giving — LENT

Like its human inhabitants, the planet earth has various ways to rid itself of pent-up pressures and to let off steam. One of the more spectacular methods of geological decompression is volcanic eruption, by which gases, heated rock, and lava flows are discharged into the atmosphere. On Sunday, May 18, 1980, Mount Saint Helens disturbed Washingtonians and residents of nearby states with a catastrophic explosion and the belching of untold tons of rock, gases, ash, and dust into the open air. This was not the first major eruption of Mount Saint Helens, nor will it likely be the last. Like other natural forces in our cosmos, volcanoes follow the rhythms of their cycles. During the days following the eruption, a fine volcanic dusting of ashes could be discerned on North Dakota windshields. We could only wonder at the destructive force which could transform masses of Pacific Northwest rock into clouds of fine ash powdering the northern prairies. Cupped in the palms of our hands with an almost reverential fascination, these dead ashes reminded us of the passing nature of all things. As long as they last, ashes give us a hint of something which once was; they point to the past.

Each year our entrance into the Lenten celebration of the Paschal Mystery is marked by ashes. Ash Wednesday introduces the season of Lent with a ritual signing of our heads with blessed ashes. This traditional devotional practice emulates the early Christian penitential customs of sprinkling ashes over the heads of a congregation to remind them of their sinfulness, and of smearing one's body or clothing with ashes as a sign of public penance. If possible, these Lenten ashes are rendered from the palms used in the previous year's celebration of Passion Sunday in Holy Week. Such a custom deftly renews the cyclic nature of liturgy by tying one year's Lent to the previous year's distinctly paschal celebration, with the physical transformation of palms into ashes.

The blackened grit and residual ash of burned palms become a sign of creational transience and a symbol of our own ephemeral and transitional participation in all life's passings. The Church minister places these ashes on participants in the rite, publicly marking them as Christian believers needing personal renewal and entering a conscious preparation for Easter grace. Ash Wednesday reveals us as fleeting echoes of the eternal Word spoken in the silence of our hearts, ceaselessly calling us back to itself. Our cinereous foreheads signify the bond we know with all created matter: we are inspirited with the breath of being until we experience life's passing in the presence of the creative force who is the source of that life and the end of our death.

Ashes speak to us in the past tense; they form the remainder of death's brief fire. The grey ashes of a home reduced to cinders remind us that all existence is transitory. The charred remains of a forest which stood in the path of a dry summer's conflagration can symbolize the great nothingness from which emerges anything which becomes something, or someone. The fine dust filling a crematory urn forces upon us all the stark realization that physiological existence is unpredictable, temporary, and subject to all the exigencies of mortality. Ashes suggest the void to us, if only subconsciously. Each one of us knows a fear of the abyss lingering at the edge of physical existence, though that fear is qualified by how we embrace life as the path to death.

Most dust is grey, nondescript and vague, like memories

of the past in relation to present experience. When the celebrant reminds us on Ash Wednesday: "Remember... you are dust and to dust you will return," we encounter the great human sadness—the question of existence toward which we are drawn and the possible answers from which we shy in our attempt to stave off the inevitability of death. Ashes and dust point to the past to the extent that they symbolize the mystery of what lies on either side of earthly existence.

But dust and ashes also represent the earth, a living ground in which the seeds of life find subsistence. Our ashened foreheads should call us all to the shared ground of being which we know in God's presence. Our existence is grounded in that presence. Ash Wednesday not only harkens to the past, but calls us toward the future and our relationship with that which seems so immeasurably beyond our comprehension and, simultaneously, so ineluctably within the spiritual fibers of our being. A Lenten smudge on the brow is a "reality touch" which brings us back to earth and grounds us in the presence of God who is always here—in the past, present, and future. Already on Ash Wednesday we see that Lenten observance is not merely reparation for past doings or remote preparation for future being, but also a matter of present living, grounded in the ethics of love.

If there is one tangible reality common to all human beings, the soil must be the most readily available and universally appreciated substance. Our existence is tied to the soil. Without dirt and its nourishing attributes, we would be sorely challenged to root around for enough edible material to stay alive. (Perhaps "rooting around" is a poorly chosen phrase to use in this context, since there are few members of the plant world which could vegetate without soil in which to root themselves.) We depend upon the earth for our very lives. And Lenten ashes remind us of that fact. We are earthbound creatures in an earthly existence. After death, our bodies break down into the chemical elements of which our natural environment is composed. Dead corpses which are not reduced to earthen dust by cremation are interred (*in-terra*), buried in the earth. "From dust to dust" runs the aphorism.

Many spiritual writers have used the image of earth or related terms to touch upon the realities of living spiritually. Like so many others throughout the centuries of Christian witness, John Cassian used the image of vegetal growth when explicating the intricacies of good and evil within the human heart. Resembling the Gospel words of Jesus about wheat and weeds (cf. Mt. 13:25f.), Cassian's remarks about virtuous living (i.e., plants flowering in the human heart) and natural vices (i.e., weeds, or tares, in the heart) give a battle plan for monastics wishing to enter the field of combat. Earth becomes the locus for spiritual struggle.

Johannes Meister Eckhart, and other proponents of what became known as the Rhineland School of Mysticism, used the image of ground to speak of the mystery of God's presence in our lives. Divine presence in the human soul became the very "ground" of being, the source of all that is. For Eckhart, spirituality was a process of rooting oneself into that inner ground.

Carmelite reformer and mystic Teresa of Avila used garden imagery to write about prayer and virtuous living. The plants prospering from the combination of soil (soul) and water (prayer) are the acts of love which give expression to a virtuous life.

The images of soil, earth, and ground have long spoken to the present realities of personal spirituality. The Ash Wednesday dusting speaks to present aspects of our Christian life, as well as to the reformation of our past and mindfulness of future death. Emphases placed on Lenten observance by Vatican Council II thankfully ground us in the present, with an eschatological eye to the future and an anamnestic ear to the past.

Lent is a time for penance, personal asceticism and fervent prayer, but its main purpose is to help people prepare for the celebration of the death and resurrection of Christ in the liturgies of Holy Week and Eastertide. The Lenten call is baptismal—centering on the immediate preparation of those to be baptized in the Easter liturgy and challenging the already baptized to grow in faith. This baptismal emphasis draws all Christians back to their roots; it grounds them deeply into the central significance of the Paschal Mystery.

During the weeks prior to the celebration of Easter, the Church urges all believers to take a good look at the virtuous plants and the hindering weeds in their spiritual ground. The baptismal roots must be well embedded and established, if the fruits of spiritual growth are to blossom. Each celebration of Eucharist is a further reentry into baptismal growth for those who consciously embrace the meaning of life found in the death and resurrection of Jesus Christ. John Cassian's field of combat is an everyday struggle for one who takes seriously the baptismal commitment that roots the Church into the ongoing cycles of death and resurrection which move around the pulse of love at the center.

Another aspect of the Lenten preparation for Easter is the stress placed upon the Word of God. Lent is to be considered a time of the liturgical cycle when we are to be particularly open to God's Word. Of course, such openness is a spiritual maxim for every day of the Church Year, but Lenten discipline embraces the discernment of and listening to God's Word with more conscious effort. This places primary emphasis on God's presence in the mundane affairs of humanity.

Meister Eckhart's ground of being finds familiar soil in

this Word-centered season. In this Word we hear the collected aspirations and inspirations of humanity coming into relationship with God who loves deeply and lives wholly.

Vatican Council II documents also emphasize the prayerful character of the Lenten season. It is a time to give oneself over to experiencing prayer in a conscientious way. Devotion to prayer furthers the Word-orientation of Lent's essentially preparatory character. With or without words, prayer is a matter of relating to the Word. The more openly we approach the phenomenon of prayer in our spiritual lives, the more authentically those lives assume paschal significance.

Teresa of Avila's garden fits well into the Lenten schema of things. Spirituality's balance between personal relationship with God (expressed in prayer) and interpersonal relationships with others (expressed in love) lays the groundwork for an authentic experience of Easter.

Lent centers on the life of conversion which each Christian believer professes by virtue of baptismal commitment. Human needs to grow, to change, to sound the depths of the heart, to plumb the unknown, and to answer the call of the Other rising from within those depths, are realized in conversional experience. In the Christian experience of conversion, we hear the call to change through a personal encounter with Christ. But many obstacles compel us to vacillate in existential tension before the prospect of conversion. We hope that somehow the illusory passage of time might effect the change from which we presently cringe. Or we mistakenly equate the conversional moment with the movement of conversion. Satisfied with the spiritual "high" of a conversional experience, we try to capture the moment by freezing it in time. Before we awaken to the thoughtlessness of our attempt to freeze the spirit, what peace we might have known escapes our grasp, like the elusive clutching of ocean sands beneath the surf. How sobering it is to undergo an overwhelming moment of conversion, only to discover that each conversional moment is but another beginning in the conversional movement!

This does not belittle the moment. During the bleakest times of desolation, often the spiritual memory of an undeniably real experience of grace at the moment of conversion keeps us spiritually intact enough to continue the long road of conversional life. There is a continuous "second" conversion on the path to spiritual growth—or psychological integrality, for that matter. Conversion must be progressive, not static. We cannot distill conversion in the vial of an isolated moment of peak-experience, hastily corked for preservation. Our spiritual freedom and unique human integrity necessitate the unique paths which each of us must travel in conversion. We hear our own calls to *metanoia* and we respond, personally and uniquely. These calls always place us on the edge of becoming. We stand before the prospect of whom we are called to become. We face our possibilities in the grace of God.

The annual pilgrimage into the Lenten season faces us with these conversional possibilities and spiritual necessities. Lent accentuates the life-rhythms of *metanoia* which weave in and out of the spiritual fabric of our lives. When Saint Benedict tells his fellow monks that every day should be Lent, he means that monks should consistently stay on the conversional path toward the celebration of Easter. Like all Christians, monks are committed to change, by virtue of their baptism. Christ's Gospel of shared life and love challenges us all to undergo the ongoing passages of conversional life. We must pass from ego-centered myopia to an other-centered vision. We must pass through ourselves and others to reach that Other, in whom we find our true selves. Lent reminds us of the importance of these passings. And the cyclic nature of these Lenten reminders resonates with the ebb and flow of our own personal spiritual conviction and psychological courage to dare the paradoxical grace of self-discovery by surrendering the status quo to renewal and change.

Sinfulness is a state of being which, to greater or lesser degrees, we all share. Perhaps it is the equalizer, second only to the condition of mortality. Like death, sin claims us all. The ashes of Lent mark our bodies as sinful bodies as well as mortal ones. What, exactly, is sin? What are the effects of being a sinful person? One of sin's effects is to obscure the image of God in our lives. Sin distances us from the center of our being; it befogs the mirror of our perception with our own breath!

Another of sin's consequences is to ignore God's presence within and around us. Sinfulness flaunts the audacity of ego in the face of divine presence; it replaces the call to love with desire's seemingly endless mutations of lusting.

A third effect of sin is to be cut off from personal relationship with God. Sinfulness constructs the barriers which prevent us from reaching out to mystery. It forces us to claw the walls of our own fashioning with the frenetic scrapings of self-preoccupation.

The penitential character of Lent is really a means by which we can focus on the self-imposed obstacles preventing us from communion with God. Whereas sin obscures the image of God, penance helps us to return to clarity of vision. It buffs the fog from the mirror. Instead of ignoring God's presence, penance tries to focus our attention on divine omnipresence. It fosters awareness of God while exposing the empty sham of self-absorption. Where sinfulness builds walls, penance helps us to shatter these illusory barriers to communication; it creates enough space for the grace of love's union to occur.

Authentic penance is not the embodiment of pious claptrap, nor a self-centered nucleus of masochistic design.

Penance is hard work, and a work of love. It speaks to our minds and bodies in ways which bring us back to earth, away from theoretical musings and expedient procrastinations. Penance sacralizes space and time by grounding us in the present experience of body and spirit. Penance accomplishes this sacralization by the flesh-and-blood ethics of love, or it is not authentically Christian.

Personal asceticism is a phenomenon found in most, if not all, religious traditions. Much of humanity's collected moments of ascetical feats and fervor could probably be catagorized as reactions from guilt or fear, propitiatory acts, tabu restrictions, or mystical prescriptions. Somehow we get it into our minds that self-inflicted suffering or the regimen of strict discipline can be channeled into a manipulation of divine power and presence. This is magic, pure and simple. Such a self-idolizing approach to God as a presence to be controlled or power to be wielded, by performing certain actions or saying fixed words, is not the response of religion. True asceticism is not concerned with the self at all, but with spiritual realities beyond the self. That is why the ascetical life is such a deceptive arena. What is designed to transcend the self by means of physical discipline and spiritual exercise, can so easily and, at times, imperceptibly degenerate into rank idolatry. Either the act of self-denial dangerously becomes an end in itself, fulfilling some need to do many things in order to escape the onus of being someone, or it idolizes the ego, boasting its reflection on itself by having it endure opposition. Well-intentioned spiritual discipline can evolve into a type of auto-voyeurism, if the focus becomes one of magic rather than one of authentic religion.

The other pole of ascetical extremity would be to equate self-denial with self-destruction. The purpose of religious self-denial is the aim of religion itself: to discover the true self in the presence of God by the transcendence of ego and self-transformation. Lent encourages us to discover, not annihilate, ourselves in relation to God. Our preparation for the Easter celebration is not a hatred for the body or physical existence within a system of "spirit versus body" dualism. The solution offered by a healthy asceticism is that self-denial is an assault upon ego's hold, but not a destruction of our unique selfhood. Lent is not enticing us into some horrid game of destruction, but prompting us to move beyond the confining strictures imposed by the ego to a greater personal freedom. The ego is obsessed with the minutiae of individual existence; ego is a solipsist. The season of preparation for Easter asks us to break away from the mirror. Asceticism, which has always been an important facet of Lent within the Church Year, asks us to be mindful of our shared humanity rather than obsessively possessed by self-serving inhumanity.

Fasting is one of the traditional ascetical practices fostered by the spirit of Lent. Although the obligatory fast has radically changed from what the Lenten fast meant only a few decades ago, the personal responsibility for anyone interested in spiritual growth to enter some type of self-denial is not to be taken lightly. Fasting remains an ascetical avenue for many of us, within and outside the Lenten season. But I think most of us limit the scope of fasting too much. We restrict our idea of fasting to the voluntary abstention from food or drink. It seems natural to connote our stomachs with the notion of fasting, but there are so many fastings which could be of greater spiritual significance for us than the curbing of our alimentary appetites.

How beneficial it would be for all concerned if Christians would enter the annual Lenten cycle of preparatory weeks by fasting from some of their more common faults! Where is the spiritual blessing of fasting from selected foods, while anger seethes within the one who fasts? The aims of spiritual discipline are moral perfection, psychological integration, and spiritual growth. If one fasts at table but festers at the eucharistic table, ascetical priorities are out of sync. Why not add refrainment from the all too facile habit of gossiping to the Lenten abstention from desserts? Ascetical hunger pains become well worth the while of the Christian who connects that physical discomfort to any conscious control of tendencies to sin with the tongue, hand, or eye. True asceticism may even ask us to fast from prayers in order to pray. Lenten spirituality is not so much concerned with the more negative aspects of ascetical self-denial as with a positive life of communion with God.

As long as the Lenten fasts blend with our human cycles of self-discovery and selfless service, our asceticism is healthy. The essential maxim of spirituality holds true: we are known by our fruits. We are known by how we love; by love will we be judged. Charity is the gauge which measures the substance behind our words, actions, and asceticisms. Ash Wednesday reminds us that we are of the earth and will return to dust upon our deaths. Lenten asceticism reminds us that there is much flesh and blood between the dust of the past and that of the future. The law of love ensures that the dust, earth, flesh, and blood are all part of communion. The wheel of our human becoming turns in the pathos and passion around us. Lent presses us to give in to love's pathos and give way to life's passion, for the wheel's turning is *metanoia*.

The long preparation for Easter is fixed within the Church Year for the accentuation of self-giving. Lent is a time for giving. Our own accent should be placed on the zealousness which characterizes the encouragement the Church offers us for our annual participation in Lenten renewal. The word "encourage" has "into the heart" as its etymological root meaning. The season of Lent speaks to the heart of spiritual struggle which underscores our time in the wilderness of the human condition. Lenten renewal encourages us to prepare for the celebration of Christ's death and resurrection, by entering our own cycles of death and resurrection through the Christian response of self-gift. In turn, we are to encourage one another in the spiritual struggle. We should go to the heart of Gospel life by giving ourselves, our time and energy, to one another. We should be fervent in the consciousness of what Christian discipleship demands of us, and enthusiastic about our response to that consciousness. Enthusiasm finds its roots in the phrases "god-possessed" and "god-possessing." Accented in Lenten spirituality, zeal is intimately connected with a vibrant relationship with God.

Our Lenten giving must be based on, and expressed in, forgiving. In anticipation of the Church's solemn entry into the Paschal Mystery, we take to heart the reconciliation with God we know in the ongoing paschal cycles of our lives. And if our lives are truly paschal, they necessarily find expression in forgiving. This forgiveness cannot fully be extended to others until we endure the breakthrough of forgiving ourselves for whatever disconcertions we might harbor within our self-hating minds. Not to forgive is to backtrack into ego's underbrush. Spiritual growth is stifled by tangled roots and parasitic creepers of egoism. To break through these entanglements, the searching heart needs to give and forgive.

The ascetics in the third and fourth century Egyptian deserts reportedly vied with one another in performing ascetical feats. Early Christian desert warfare was a reality! Lent does not ask us to compete in our asceticisms, except perhaps in the area of striving to be first in serving others. We could call this gift the grace of anticipating and meeting others' needs. When such a grace becomes second nature— when we give and forgive automatically—we are very close to the Kingdom of God. Perhaps what annoys us about holy persons is that their untiring ability to give of themselves shames our own hidden corners—ego's haunts. But Lent fashions saints, and Lent is for us all.

The first Preface for Lent in the Church's Sacramentary concerns itself with God's gift to us:

> Each year you give us this joyful season
> when we prepare to celebrate the paschal mystery
> with mind and heart renewed.
> You give us a spirit of loving reverence for you, our Father,
> and of willing service to our neighbor.
>
> As we recall the great events that gave us new life in Christ, you bring the image of Your Son to perfection within us.
> (Preface, Lent 1)

The giftedness of Lenten spirituality centers on the meaning of our existence, the essence of life. This is not metaphysical speculation, but the marrow of real "ontic" giving. Lent is a time to give of our unique selves to others, regardless of the tonality in which the music of our lives expresses itself. There are no major or minor keys in essential Gospel living, merely sound giving form to our hearts dancing above the abyss in a tremulant awareness of sacred presence.

IV
A Time for Dying — HOLY WEEK

Rarely, it seems, does the phrase "quiet before the storm" actually refer to atmospheric conditions. We use it proverbially to speak of the calm preceding a psychological disorder or personal agitation of some sort. People about to undergo the full brunt of tornadic activity have noticed how an eerie quiet pervades the atmosphere just before meteorological hell breaks loose. This phenomenon is due, no doubt, to changes in pressure, but the proverbial usage of "quiet before the storm" refers to pressure changes of another sort!

A slight twist of phrase can describe my personal experience of storms: quiet during the storm. Blessed with a philosophical bent since childhood, I have been dubbed a dreamer by friends and religious confreres. I am drawn to storms like an astronomer to the telescope. The more violent the storm, the more awed I become by the power of a greater presence around us and within us. Storms bring out an awareness level that forces me to step back and observe the chaos which pervades our "well-ordered" lives and, from within and without, the barriers we construct to order that chaos. I am reminded of my own vulnerability, as well as purpose for my life in my personal dependencies and uncertainties. By the inescapable display of unleashed violence beyond the walls, storms can still the inner turmoil so often unrecognized.

The annual celebration of Holy Week inevitably accords me an inner quiet amid all the noises within the walls. It matters little where I might be during Holy Week. Life's noises are always well in evidence, but the grace which quiets my heart, from the palm-waving procession on Passion Sunday to the fire ceremony opening the Easter Vigil, is also predictably at hand to turn my pensive nature toward the contemplation of death. In the parish of my childhood, Holy Week was marked by statues and crosses draped in purple silk, wooden clackers replacing the usual sanctuary bells, and every available cassock brought out of mothballs for the four elaborate candlelight processions in the church. Already then, the mystique of Holy Week gripped me with the reality of Christ's suffering and death.

During Naval Basic Training, a bout with acute tonsillitis landed me in the ear, nose, and throat ward of the base medical facility. One night some corpsmen delivered a delirious seaman to our ward, billeting him to the hospital cot diagonal to mine. By morning the unfortunate man had died without regaining consciousness, and we found ourselves quarantined for two weeks to prevent an outbreak of the nemesis of boot camps—spinal meningitis. Holy Week spent in quarantine was no less captivating for its lack of purple coverings and the smell of incense. Perhaps life's paschal realities came to the fore even more vividly than usual, since my own physical survival was suddenly very much at issue! Despite the bustle of ward life and the vented frustrations of quarantined sailors, I experienced the quieting time of Holy Week.

Years later, I spent Holy Week in private retreat at Our Lady of Gethsemani Abbey in Trappist, Kentucky. The liturgies were impressive and spiritually nourishing, but I treasured most the times of solitude in the gardens. When I found Father Louis (Thomas) Merton's grave in the monastic cemetery, a cardinal flew overhead in a flash of red. At that moment I experienced an intuitive understanding of Good Friday which I could not begin to put into words, though I tried to do so in a poem.

Regardless of where I have been, the experience of Holy

Week has always seemed to be a pivotal time of life for me. Perhaps I measure out my life in Holy Weeks, like J. Alfred Prufrock does with coffee spoons. I do know that I have been most real in the stillness of this time, and thankfully still am so. The quiet of Holy Week arrives like the early morning hints of light in the pre-dawn glow, bringing with it an assurance of radiancy and illumination. But the reality of dying is not glossed over by the promise of rising. There could be no Easter without the Golgotha which gave it meaning. Perhaps the solemn proclamation of Christ's Passion on the Sunday of Holy Week is the constant factor which has consistently quieted my personal unrest and pivoted my unfocused heart to a contemplation of the paschal realities in my own life. From the moment during the Church Year when Jesus sets his sights on Jerusalem, I enter that pilgrimage of ascent which more clearly centers on my responsibility to let go whatever hinders movement —my assent to the ascent.

One of the thematic threads running through the Gospel accounts of Jesus' life, just prior to the events surrounding his betrayal and execution, is his ascent to the holy city of Jerusalem. Mirroring the ascents of generations of pious Jews making their pilgrim journeys to the city, his own "going up" to Jerusalem took Jesus into the core of Jewish piety, as well as to the crux of meaning for his earthly life among us.

His entry into Jerusalem is met with an enthusiastic welcome by disciples and the crowd which had gathered for Passover purification. Some placed their cloaks on the road while others cut branches or reeds to mark his passage. The fourth Gospel tells us that the crowd obtained palm branches and met Christ in procession.

> They cried out: "Hosanna!
> Blessed is he who comes in the name of the Lord!
> Blessed is the King of Israel!" (Jn. 12:13).

How this messianic reference must have offended pious Pharisees and disturbed the politically-minded leaders of the Jewish people! Who could say where such inappropriate and imprudent actions might lead? Who could predict the political outcome of such preposterous events? Jesus Christ entered the city, facing the inevitable encounter with the paranoia and outright hatred which had festered within the Jewish leaders and had followed Jesus during his short-lived public ministry.

The synoptic accounts relate that Jesus followed up his triumphal entrance into Jerusalem with his upbraiding of the merchants in the temple area, further upsetting Jewish officials.

> Then he entered the temple and began ejecting the traders saying:
> "Scripture has it,
> 'My house is meant for a house of prayer'
> but you have made it a 'den of thieves.' "
> He was teaching in the temple area from day to day. The chief priests and scribes meanwhile were looking for a way to destroy him, as were the leaders of the people, but they had no idea how to achieve it, for indeed the entire populace was listening to him and hanging on his words (Lk. 19:45-48).

The crowds were listening to Jesus. They were open to his words against injustice and his actions which flaunted a spiritual freedom the Jewish leaders could not ignore. The people were receptive to the encouragement Christ offered the *anawim*—all the social, religious, and political outcasts of the people. They were responsive to his wonder-working presence. They would hang on his words as they waited for the Galilean rumors they had heard about Jesus to gain some substance in Jerusalem.

But somewhere along the Jerusalem road, the crowds stopped listening. They closed off Jesus, rejecting his message and even promoting his execution. For whatever reasons—mob psychology, political expediency, religious pressure, petty jealousy—the crowds stopped listening when it became uncomfortable or risky. They exchanged their fronds of palms for thorn branches, as the desolation of human folly took them into the wasteland of the hardened heart. And if that heart is hardened enough, all the world's passion cannot penetrate its veneer. Expediency prides itself on its passionlessness.

The Jewish festival cycle had run its course, and the time for Passover turned their minds to the ritual meal. Like other pious Jews, Jesus and his disciples gathered to break Passover bread and to remember the spiritual journey of God's people. During the course of the meal, Christ surprised his disciples by wrapping a cloth around his waist and, kneeling in front of each one of them in turn, washing and drying their feet as a sign of service. "Do you understand what I just did for you?" (Jn. 13:12), Jesus asked the disciples gathered around the Passover table. He tied the realities of mutual service and shared love to the breaking of bread and sharing the cup. This foot washing service performed by Christ at the memorial meal was inseparably connected with the profound service he would soon render humanity at the place of crucifixion.

In the Upper Room, humanity experienced a meal of meaning and communion of purpose which reach down through the centuries of the world's passion to our own day. Whenever we break bread at the eucharistic meal, we are obligated to live the commandment of love expressed in the act of washing feet. Around the Lord's Table, we celebrate what it means to be a Christian believer. What is faith in action if not a communion of hearts united by their oneness experienced in Christ? How can Christians possibly refuse to break down their barriers and be reconciled with one another, particularly when they form that circle of fellowship around the eucharistic altar? When Jesus performed his act of service within the framework of the Jewish Passover meal and uttered his words about body and blood in connection with the bread and cup, he realized the eschatological thrust of the original Passover.

Stemming from the mystery celebrated in that Jerusalem Upper Room, Eucharist celebrates Jesus' own exodus from alienation to life with God. Though they did not understand the significance of this meal, the disciples' later commemorations of this event centered on the new salvific reality experienced in Jesus' self-gift, represented in the eucharistic gifts. The one bread broken for all and the one cup shared by all became the bearers of Christ's self-gift, prophetic signs of the New Passover. Eucharistically, we enter the death and resurrection of the Lord. Through its shared service, the Christian community is called upon to *be* eucharistic sacrifice. Eucharistic bread and wine are the bearers and means of Christ's self-gift to us, as well as our own self-giving service to others.

The Paschal Mystery founds the Church, while the rhythms of our paschal, eucharistic lives focus on that Church-event where Christ actively unifies people. Our own sacramental cycles of breaking bread and sharing the cup of reconciliation bring the disparate elements of our lives together into communion. But the key to authenticity in our Church communion can be traced back to the washing of feet. The covenant is truly entered through the door of service. Who would have thought that the passage to the Messianic Banquet would be by way of the service door?

The festive eucharistic meal celebrated on the evening of Holy Thursday ends soberly with a blue note of austerity. The altar cloths and other embellishments are removed from the table on which the annual commemoration of the Lord's Supper had been celebrated, revealing a barren, austere plane to which we are unaccustomed. After all, the celebration of Eucharist is a daily sacramental encounter with the Paschal Mystery during this interim between the two comings of Christ. But the cloths are removed, mirroring the self-stripping undergone by Jesus after that evening meal with his disciples. The church sanctuary is bereft, like our hearts which somehow remember what our minds cannot imagine. The lamp is extinguished and we are challenged to find our way in and out of the darkened garden beyond the veil of sensibility.

The presence of anguish and suffering in our world is a universal human experience. When Christ came to grips with an inevitable clash with Jewish leaders and his ultimate rejection by the Jewish people, he sorted out his thoughts and emotions in the garden near the Kidron brook. Jesus' prayer to be relieved of his anguish reflected the apprehension of a suffering humanity confronted with the prospect of death. Death is always lurking behind the stage, waiting for time's unconcern to snuff out the lights and lower the curtain. It would be unrealistic to view the world other than as breathing the air of suffering, for pain is an inevitable condition of mortality. Diminishment is everywhere we turn. While the universe may be physically expanding in space, our own diminishing is part of its spiritual expansion. And each one of us shares the human consciousness that existence is really a matter of dying. The wise and holy ones among us know that the quality of such existence is intimately determined by how we enter the processes of dying.

Our lives may be suffering lives, but what progress we make toward psychological integration and spiritual synthesization comes by way of that suffering. We grow at the expense of many failures, wounds, and deaths. We expand through the grace of diminishing. In the garden of Gethsemani, Jesus Christ prayed that he be spared the bitter cup of betrayal, rejection, condemnation, and execution, but he gained the personal strength to undergo such extreme wounds only by his abandonment to the Father's will. Matthew and Mark wrote that Jesus prayed three times in this vein: "My Father, if it is possible, let this cup pass me by. Still, let it be as you would have it, not as I.... My Father, if this cannot pass me by without my drinking it, your will be done!" (Mt. 26:39-42).

The crucial significance of Jesus' Mount of Olives experience for our participation in the ongoing Paschal Mystery is that we must trust our suffering is tied to what being human means, and that surrender to faith in God's love and will for us transfigures our deaths into life.

Pain discovers its ultimate consummation in death. The Christian way of overcoming death is to find God in the dying. In death, each of us has the opportunity to attain union with God. Each moment of dying we encounter—each Gethsemani garden we endure—is a further possibility for communion. If we try to ignore the suffering or deny the dying, then the pain becomes *our* pain and *remains* our pain. Even stoical endurance can merely be a drill of will in staving off opportunities for grace. As long as suffering remains personal domain, we are trapped inside our own walls. Though at times it may seem a very powerful force, self-will is essentially a meaningless exercise in shadow boxing.

Refusal to recognize the cycles of dying in life denies the very movement of life. There are many shades to death's denial, but the result is always an unmoving, nebulous wasteland of grey. We can ingeniously discover means for avoiding cycles of dying, but the avoidance only entrenches our need to escape self-confinement. The universal process of dying is but the transformation from life to life.

Unfortunately, only too often we become the direct or indirect causes of others' sufferings, as if the complex process of existing does not already experience enough inherent suffering! The inhumanity of our wounding each other helps neither the human cycles of birthing nor those of dying. Evil is only interested in perpetuating itself on an altar of destruction within the niche of complacency. Compassion is the instrument for demolishing the idol of self-preservation. To reach out to another in pain—to suffer with that other—enables the transformative power of dying to self to experience the covenant of eternal life among us. Compassion can change a death rattle to the pangs of birth, for life is the very pith of dying.

Christian community challenges us all to stay awake during the moments of Gethsemani around us. Spiritual authenticity demands that we not deny the willing spirit life, simply because the mind knows a weakness for evasion. We are fools if we try to deny those gardens within us. We become our own betrayers, and what hangs in the balance swings from the Judas tree of self-loathing and despair.

Good Friday is the hinge of the liturgical year, the axis on which turn the wheels of Christian human becoming. On this day of the Easter Triduum celebration, we commemorate that pivotal event for humanity when Jesus Christ died. Jesus let go what control he had over persons and events in order to suffer a humiliating and horrid death. At the time of the Passover, he saw himself as the sacrifice of a new Passover: humanity sacrificed—made holy—in the will of his Father.

Perhaps most of us find it difficult to understand why death by crucifixion should be the crucial event of salvation. Of course, without the subsequent resurrection of Jesus, we would find the cross impossible to comprehend. The cross is a graphic symbol for human nature's inhumanity toward itself. And the way of the cross becomes a powerful avenue by which women and men can judge the authenticity of their own journeys toward God. The extent of physical suffering is not the issue, nor are the particular circumstances surrounding pain the point in question. The movement of surrender motivated by compassion is the momentum on the road to Golgotha. Salvation in Jesus Christ comes to us not because he lived and died, but because he lived and died for *us*. The cross has become a symbol of untiring and devoted service of others. The sacrifice on the cross is humanity made whole again. The way of the cross is the path of life for all who live their lives in the service of others.

But what was the crucifixion of Jesus to those onlookers who gathered around the Hill of Skulls? To the Romans occupying the land and carrying out the death sentence, was the cross an end to some fool or fanatic? To the Jewish leaders who had hoped for this day with a vengeance, was this cross a cause for sighs of political and religiose relief? To the disciples who had the courage to risk showing their faces at the execution, was Christ Crucified the disappointing climax to messianic fervor, or another example of a good man undone by the authorities? And what about all those powerless and purposeless outcasts whom he had cured and comforted, nourished and enlivened? Was Christ the punchline to some horrible joke played upon the masses? It is a useful kataphatic meditation to put ourselves in the places of those onlookers, not so much to understand more clearly the different mindsets at Golgotha, as to perceive ourselves in those onlookers.

All of us go through cycles of dying and rising, as well as refusing to die or rise. In the paschal realities of daily rubbing shoulders, the Crucified Lord is before, behind, and within us. The recognition of Jesus' lordship should make our dyings more unconstrained, but our acknowledgment of suffering as an integral and upbuilding part of paschal life should aid us in fashioning this world as a place of compassion and communion.

When Christians gather on Good Friday to venerate the cross of Christ, the celebrant invites the people to worship by singing: "This is the wood of the cross, on which hung the Savior of the world." The cross is a marker for us, marking the crossroads of all our unique pathways to God—and to one another, for that matter. Christ is in the watching, birthing, giving, and dying, as well as in all the life-cycles we encounter anew throughout our lives together. The cross is also a staff of support, a crutch for our weaknesses, but when it is planted in receptive ground, it blossoms into the tree of life like a desiccated desert branch springing to life in the long-awaited rain. Our roots lie exposed on this tree, rather than beneath it. The suffering inherent in the human condition comes from this exposure. But we always do well to remember that the tree itself is anchored in the love of God, an anchorage which reaches toward the heavens and embraces our cosmos in that reaching.

In the closing remarks of his Epistle to the Galatians, Paul writes: "May I never boast of anything but the cross of our Lord Jesus Christ! Through it, the world has been crucified to me and I to the world" (Gal. 6:14). At the crossroads of crucifixion, humanity has found the bond of love which cements our sufferings, one to another. In that solidarity, we accept the difficult truth that the fullness of life can only be attained by the cycles of death we undergo during our spiritual growth. Our paschal awareness—transformation in Christ—is the glory we celebrate during Holy Week. This is the glory of transformation, without which there can be no glory. Good Friday is not a purely ritualistic action of vicarious religious experience, but a real entry into the Paschal Mystery.

Each one of us encounters the cross in many ways. Our salvation lies in the qualitative turns we take on the cruxes of our becoming. For the grace is in the turning, and the turning can be so graceful, if only we let go our hesitancies.

V
A Time for Rising — EASTER

In Sanskrit, the term "mandala" denotes circle and center. Using such geometric forms as the square and circle, the mandala is designed to link humanity with the cosmos. Mandala is a symbol of life's flow; it evokes the cosmic circle of celestial spheres, the seasons, cycles, being. Found in many cultures with a delightful array of variations, the mandala form roots itself in the essence of reality. It constitutes at its center the *axis mundi*, the cosmic core which orders the chaos for those who find this center.

When I was a child, the weather program for one of our local television stations used a modified face of a compass as its logo, picturing the four cardinal points in a circle. Already, at that early age, I correlated the seasons with the four directions into a rotating seasonal wheel: north (cold) with winter, east (rising sun) with spring, south (heat) with summer, west (setting sun) with autumn. I now know that the circle of seasons is a mandala to me, ordering the natural changes I experience in weather and climate into a wheel of awareness and awe. And I stand at that wheel's hub, making the connections I must make and trying to let the rhythms of my own existence resonate with those cosmic rhythms of humanity discovering its God.

When the seasonal wheel turns from winter to spring, the warmth of light increases as the days lengthen. What lay frozen and hidden by winter's effacing cover, now emerges with quickened life. Springtime is nature's quickener. With the melting snows heralding an end to winter's time of death and dormancy, the ground begins to thaw.

New life appears in the shoots and buds of another year's greening. Spring is a season of return. Migrating birds return to the woods and fields. Other animals return to activity from hibernation's dormant wintering. Even insects return to their accustomed haunts to greet a less resilient humanity which takes a tentative step into the open air.

Like autumn, spring is essentially a time of transition and change. It is our passage from winter to summer when we celebrate the new cycle of planting and growth. Liturgically, Easter fittingly celebrates the springtime of our own spiritual becoming. As the migratory birds return to familiar nesting grounds, at Easter we return to the miracle of new life in resurrection. Easter light lengthens our hope, increasing our awareness of the grace which thaws our hardened hearts and quickens our deadened spirits. Eastertide marks *the* journey of passage to which each of us is called on the turning wheel of Christian human becoming.

Though there are many crucial moments celebrated on the Church calendars' cycle of feasts and seasons, the solemnity of Easter is surely the most pivotal of them all. Had the ugliness and suffering of Jesus' crucifixion not been transformed by God into the enlivening power and glory of the resurrection, the Church of Christ could never have begun its pilgrim journey with success. And why would it have begun such a journey in the first place? The Easter event of the Paschal Mystery has absolute bearing upon and central significance for all that we become and all that we can accomplish in the name of Jesus Christ. Each mystery of Christ we celebrate during the liturgical year is illuminated by Easter light and reflects the essential centrality of the Paschal Mystery.

After passing through the passion of Holy Week with its spiritual sign of dying, we enter the Easter Mystery with its spiritual sign of rising to new life. Personally, I find the liturgy of the Easter Vigil the most impressive, aesthetic and religiously encompassing celebration of the entire Church Year. The blessing of the fire and the light ceremony which precede the liturgy of the Word are rich with symbolism and evocative of our commonality in the spiritual search. The symbols of fire and light are archetypal symbols which speak to us of life and revelation, among other realities. Jesus himself said: "I have come to light a fire on the earth. How I wish the blaze were ignited! I have a baptism to receive. What anguish I feel till it is over! Do you think I have come to establish peace on the earth? I assure you, the contrary is true; I have come for division" (Lk. 12:49-51). Jesus Christ ignited that Gospel fire with the message of new life and universal love.

John the Baptist had told the crowds who were wondering if John might be the Messiah: "I am baptizing you in water, but there is one to come who is mightier than I. I am not fit to loosen his sandal strap. He will baptize you in the Holy Spirit and in fire" (Lk. 3:16). Jesus came to light that fire, as John had predicted—a fire of division, as Jesus had foretold.

The Gospel fire separates darkness from light and death from life. Those who choose the Easter light of Christ, choose life. The Prologue to the Gospel of John reads, in part:

> Whatever came to be in him,
> found life,
> life for the light of men.
> The light shines on in darkness,
> a darkness that did not overcome it (Jn. 1:4-5).

These themes of light and life are woven into the fabric of John's entire Gospel, but appear most succinctly in Jesus' words:

> "I am the light of the world.

No follower of mine shall ever walk in darkness;
no, he shall possess the light of life" (Jn. 8:12).

When we light and bless the new fire on Holy Saturday—when we light the Easter candle from the blessed flame and proclaim the *Exsultet*—we process in the light of our lives and live in the unbroken procession of Easter celebrations of this light. From the "Light of Christ" to the solemn dismissal, the music of the Easter Vigil celebrates this life we know in the presence of the Risen Lord.

Another powerful symbol of life we encounter during the Easter Vigil is the water for the baptismal liturgy. In baptism we are drawn into the Paschal Mystery of Christ, incorporated into Christ Crucified and Glorified. We bless ourselves with the Easter water, renewing our baptismal commitment to Christ and to one another. Easter water reminds us of the bonds we share with each other, the unity of Christian community. Paul reminds us that we are a new creation in the waters of baptism, where we put on Christ. He sees Christian life as a pilgrimage in baptismal perspective.

Baptism is coextensive with the entire life of the Christian believer. Baptism into Christ is baptism into the death and the resurrection of Christ. We die to sin and rise with Christ, animated by the Holy Spirit hovering over the Easter waters of the new creation. John speaks more of being born of water and the Spirit or being children of God than of dying to sin or being a new person. But the Easter event we celebrate in fire and water, with Alleluias and bells, and through an anamnestic journey of scriptural texts relating to Christ, is a witness to all these spiritual realities. In the Easter Mystery we honor birth and death, as well as all the birthings and dyings in the interim between the two. Most of all, we rejoice in the rising to new life which is our promise in Christ.

Easter light calls us to the waters of baptism which, in turn, call us to a continuous participation in our own divinization. Eastern Church Fathers, as well as mystical writers in both the Eastern and Western Christian traditions, have stressed the human person's divinization by which he or she comes to share in the divine life through the grace of Christ, and attains union with God in relation to the Risen Lord. Sacramental life witnesses to the present reality of this participation—this ongoing divinization—enabling us to become one with the Father and the Son in the life of the Holy Spirit.

This divinization is a gift from God whose initiative manifests an enduring love for humanity, offering us a share in divine life through the revelation of the life-giving Word, Jesus Christ. This sharing is gratuitous, in no way merited. We respond to God's loving gift of eternal life with our faith in Christ who spent his public ministry manifesting the very life of his Father. Our baptismal faith commitment to God is a movement of surrender that we might rise with Christ. We learn to loosen the hold of our individual wills and to allow room for God's will in our lives, if we really want to become God's children, to share God's life, to be divinized.

Divinization's participation in the life and love of God is an ongoing movement of a person into fuller union with the divine. In this union the believer experiences life's fullness—eternal life as an already present reality. Each of us is called by baptism to participation in this union with divine life. We glorify God by manifesting God's life and love. Our rising to new life in Christ is *the* Christian witness. It is a call to life and to love, an invitation to experience the gift of God's loving presence and the eternity of God's life. This call is especially an Easter summons to express that divine reality by sharing it with others in concrete ways. By loving others, we become the epiphany of God's love in the world: God's grandeur.

The First Epistle of John gives us insight into some of the particulars of divinization through which we must pass in our personal and communal risings with Christ. "God is light; in him there in no darkness" (1 Jn. 1:5), writes the author. In this Easter light, we are enabled to find our way and follow the path clearly marked for us by Christ. To be in the light means to be in union with God, and carries with it love's imperative.

> The man who continues in the light
> is the one who loves his brother;
> there is nothing in him to cause a fall (1 Jn. 2:10).

Loving one another is an expression of dwelling in Easter light—loving openly, in the light of God's truth. This light becomes for us an expression of what divinization means. The baptized believer must live in the light, live that light, and become a living symbol of God's love in the world. This dwelling in Easter light is contrasted with the darkness where we cannot share God's love. Although the darkness is passing away in the power and glory of the Risen Christ, John says those who refuse to acknowledge Christ still grope around in the darkness. Refusing love's call, they espouse hatred:

> But the man who hates his brother is in darkness.
> He walks in shadows,
> not knowing where he is going,
> since the dark has blinded his eyes (1 Jn. 2:11).

Love is the key to divinization. To claim union with God without selfless love is a sham. The power which seeks to control, possess, and manipulate people or things builds a wall which the light of God's love does not penetrate. This wall is constructed in hatred, suspicion, envy, and greed.

> If anyone loves the world,
> the Father's love has no place in him,
> for nothing that the world affords

comes from the Father....
And the world with its seductions is passing away
but the man who does God's will
endures forever (1 Jn. 2:15-17).

To be "of God," the baptized Christian must overcome the world. God's light and love are the realities which enable us to do so. Divinized humanity is in the world, yet not of the world; it is of God, having God's word within it. The love which a divinized person expresses is not love directed toward things, powers, or self, but a love of God experienced in Christ and shared with others.

We share in God's love and divine life through the power and grace of the Risen Lord. God's indwelling within us expresses a love which moves out into the fellowship of shared existence and divinization. The community in God's Spirit becomes the locus of God's loving activity and the visible witness to eternal life. 1 John assures us that we have three witnesses to Christ's coming: water, blood, and the Spirit. Jesus Christ was baptized, lived among us and died on the cross. We now share in that living presence of God's love among us in the sacraments of Baptism and Eucharist. Through the power of the Holy Spirit in the sacraments, we share in eternal life. They are witnesses to our very divinization. We become God's children by sharing in that relationship with God we experience in Christ who came to share God's life and love with us. By our faith in the Risen Christ, we rise to become God's children—divinized.

When anyone acknowledges that Jesus
is the Son of God,
God dwells in him
and he in God (1 Jn. 4:15).

At the moment of baptism we are reborn in the eternal life of God. With the practical living out of this moment in many moments throughout life, we live a baptismal commitment to Christ and the reality of God's love. Baptism is the sign of our union with God; in baptism we are born of God, becoming God's children. Being born of God is not merely an eschatological reality with an eye to some future union with the divine. Such a rebirth places present demands upon us who are being divinized. We strive to rise with Christ as we suffer the many deaths to self. In the end, the ultimate implications of our divinization remain a mystery. We live in Christian hope which is grounded in our faith in Jesus Christ and the experience of God's love which he manifested in his life, death, and resurrection. Our hope motivates our participation in the divinization of ourselves and of those around us.

God's life in us and our own abiding in God denote an ongoing reality. Christian life is lived in hope—a faithful stance which responds to love's imperatives. Divinization is not static, but a dynamic movement in and toward union with God. Animated by the Spirit's promptings, we experience a vital union with God and God's children. God lives in us and, in response to this indwelling, we learn to surrender our will to God's will by following the example of Jesus Christ.

> The way we can be sure we are in union
> with him
> is for the man who claims to abide in
> him
> to conduct himself just as he did (1 Jn. 2:5-6).

We are to walk in Easter light and, in that light, be divinized.

If God is both light and love, then our faith enlightened by God must be witnessed in loving. Likewise, our love must always be animated by authentic faith. Our love for each other is real only to the extent that it expresses God's love for us, since God is love. The bond of unity in Christian communal fellowship is the divine love manifested to us in Christ, love which we return to God through lived charity for one another. The religious life of the Christian is nothing less than a participation in God's life. Love itself opens up to an ever greater capacity to love. God lives in us to the extent to which we give ourselves over to love of one another. We cannot love God without loving others. We cannot fully love others without surrendering ourselves to God's love. We must know ourselves as lovable because God lives in us. Our divinization asks us to open ourselves unqualifiedly to love's demands. The Easter community of Christ must be involved with one another. Easter fellowship is life itself because it expresses the gift of eternal life—the divine life which we share. Love of God and neighbor become the very tests of divinization.

> One who has no love for the brother he
> has seen
> cannot love the God he has not seen (1 Jn. 4:20).

Love's demands are such that we must love as we are loved. Mutual love becomes an obligation as well as an opportunity. Love must be lived in concrete acts of charity. Walking in Easter light places ethical demands on us. To say that we love without expressing that love is an illusion. We cannot claim to live in God if we ignore the responsibility of sharing that life in moral obligations to one another.

> I ask you, how can God's love survive
> in a man
> who has enough of this world's goods
> yet closes his heart to his brother
> when he sees him in need? (1 Jn. 3:17).

Our divinization is found in the sharing of God's life we know in love. If love cannot be translated into responsible personal action, then it is not true love; it is not of God.

We experience the gift of divine life in the Easter fellowship of Church. Within the context of Church we celebrate the living presence of the Risen Christ in a vital communion with God. In Christ we already participate in eternal life.

> The testimony is this:
> God gave us eternal life,
> and this life is in his Son (1 Jn. 5:11).

Our sacramental life nourishes us with the desire to be one with God. As celebration of the Risen Christ's living presence among us, the sacraments are signs of our divinization. In the resurrection we have the fullness of being. Jesus' resurrection from death has transformed the world, offering to all persons the potentiality for divinization. With the Risen Christ, we are enabled to share in God's eternal life. And in that sharing of God's life, we are all called to participate in the divinization of the world around us. But divinization's true potential can only be realized by the freedom we know in our self-abandonment to God's living presence. We cannot rise in Easter grace if we continue to weigh ourselves down with heavy hearts, bent on a tomb.

The friends and early disciples of Jesus found themselves heavy of heart after the crucifixion and burial of the Lord. But Christ transformed their mourning and trepidation into joy and tranquillity with words of peace and encouragement when he appeared to them after his resurrection. Whether talking to Mary Magdalene in the garden, to apostles in the Upper Room, to his disciples on the road to Emmaus or on a Galilean hillside, Jesus' post-resurrectional appearances pulled the early Christian believers out of themselves and called them into an Easter light where they could rise to an awareness of eternal life. The disciples rose to these occasions and perceived their vocation to be an evangelical sharing of life and love. In time, they understood that faith in Jesus Christ would not only entail a kenotic stripping—self-emptying participation in Christ's suffering and death—but also the miraculous gift of eternal life in the Risen Lord's resurrection.

Like these apostles and early disciples of Jesus, we too are invited to participate in the gift of resurrection. Though our contemporary "Easter duty" may be an obligation to be reconciled to the Church fellowship and the Lord's Table sacramentally, we should never forget that, as Easter people, our most essential responsibility is to recognize the Risen Lord where he may be found and to embrace that recognition with love. Do our hearts not burn within us when we experience God's loving presence in the person of Christ: in God's Word, in prayer, in the celebrations of Church, in the transforming love we give to one another? Are not our eyes opened to recognize Christ in the breaking of bread, in the mysteries of birthing and dying, in the intimate sharing of joy and suffering, in the light of Christian witness we see in our brothers and sisters? Are we not impelled to share this great gift of recognition with others, to mingle the mystery of our own walking in Easter light with the mysteries of those around us? And in this commingling of mysteries, do we not stand amazed by God who gives us conviction nurtured in hope and articulated in love? Like the two disciples on the road to Emmaus, do not our hearts compel us to turn to the Lord and say, "Stay with us" (Lk. 24:29)? Be our light, Lord, that flame of love to be fueled with our lives' breath, shared unto exhaustion.

Our lives of divinization will intensify in God's love when we allow ourselves to know the grace of rising with the Lord as deeply as we experience our moments of dying with the Lord. These times of rising are ours by virtue of the Easter light radiating from the Paschal Mystery. We are challenged to step into this light, recognize the Lord, and walk with him where he journeys. We must be ready always to pick up life's pieces and begin the journey anew. During moments fully centered on the possibilities of eternal life, we can be transformed in Christ. As we progress on our path of divinization, we may be able to realize the hope which Paul prayed for the Church in Ephesus:

> May Christ dwell in your hearts through faith, and may charity be the root and foundation of your life. Thus you will be able to grasp fully, with all the holy ones, the breadth and length and height and depth of Christ's love, and experience this love which surpasses all knowledge, so that you may attain to the fullness of God himself (Eph. 3:17-19).

In the Risen Christ we celebrate the greatest opening to the Sacred which human history has witnessed. He becomes the threshold of our new awareness that oneness with God is not only a possibility, but reality. We must respond to the gift which Jesus Christ promised to all who believe in his words and embrace his Gospel of truth, selfless service, and passionate love. The promised gift is life: "I give them eternal life, and they shall never perish" (Jn. 10:28). We are still living in that Easter light of the Risen Lord, a light which fills us with God's grace. It is our firm belief that, if we walk in this light, we will have eternal life. Our awesome responsibility is to glow with this light, to be transfigured in the redemptive presence of Christ—our most precious gift. If we really want to rise in this Easter light and to participate in God's eternal life, we must fearlessly learn to live freely and love profoundly, without wasting our lives trying to differentiate the loving from the living.

VI
A Time for Believing —
ASCENSION/PENTECOST

The liturgical season of Ascensiontide is often greeted with joy as a complement to Paschaltide and a foreshadowing of the Pentecost event, but for me it brings back memories of one of the singularly most formative experiences of my young life. When it happened, all those years ago, I only knew the event to be a devastating experience of abandonment, and, in one sense, I was never quite the same person after that traumatic episode. My best friend, whom I had admired and trusted for years, suddenly decided that our friendship was no longer expedient. He abruptly ended it with no real explanation.

There is much to say for not putting all of one's emotional eggs into one basket, and I soon learned to invest my time and energy in more than one relationship of consequence. But the pain I suffered as a direct result of the experience of abandonment was formative, affecting how I have related (or not related) with people to this day. There is nothing like "getting burned" in personal relationships to teach us valuable lessons about ourselves. When our emotional investment is tossed back into our faces and we must look into the mirror for understanding, how we react when confronted with rejection or abandonment will determine how successfully we grow through the experience into persons who can know themselves as vulnerable, accept that fact, and keep on relating.

I would not be surprised to discover that some of the apostles and early disciples of Jesus Christ had experienced abandonment, in some way, during those weeks and years following Jesus' ascension to the Father. They may not have consciously thought of their experiences as abandonment or rejection, but surely they must have felt something of the sort! Mark's Gospel account tells us that, "the Lord Jesus was taken up into heaven and took his seat at God's right hand" (Mk 16:19). In Luke, we read: "As he blessed them, he left them, and was taken up to heaven" (Lk 24:51). In the sequel to his Gospel account, Luke elaborates on Jesus' ascension:

> No sooner had he said this than he was lifted up before their eyes in a cloud which took him from their sight.
> They were still gazing up into the heavens when two men dressed in white stood beside them. "Men of Galilee," they said, "why do you stand here looking up at the skies? This Jesus who has been taken from you will return, just as you saw him go up into the heavens" (Acts 1:9-11).

Regardless of how the event actually happened, Jesus' ascension inescapably placed upon his friends and loved ones the burden of the human condition: consciously dealing with mortality. Although Jesus did not abandon his followers, but returned to them in the power of resurrection, the Ascension removed Jesus from their midst in a way which forced them to seek and to experience his presence among themselves in new ways.

We are told that the early Christian community which formed around the apostles in Jerusalem devoted themselves to communal sharing of goods, the breaking of bread, and prayer. Many, if not all of them, expected the imminent return of the glorified Christ to their midst and the end of the world to occur within their lifetime. Bereft of the physical presence of a teaching, healing, and reconciling Jesus, some disciples suffered the despair of abandonment and parted company with the believers. Others took their pain to prayer, transforming their desolation at Jesus' departure into fervent hope for his return in glory. The departure of Jesus and the experience of God's Holy

Spirit among the early Christian believers encouraged them to peer into the evangelical mirror and to form a community bonded in love. Christ's ascension was formative of ecclesial awareness, setting the stage for the Holy Spirit's work of love.

The Church's liturgical celebration of the Ascension is not merely an isolated moment during the Easter season, historically wedged between the solemnities of Easter and Pentecost. The Ascension is integral to the Paschal Mystery. We celebrate Christ's glorification in power and presence. Jesus' surrender to the Father's will is complete; he is taken to the Father. But the Ascension is not only a celebration of Christ Glorified; it is also a celebration of Church itself. We often think of Pentecost as *the* Church-event, but we should remember that the Ascension readied the believers to open themselves to an experience of Pentecost. The Church encourages believers to ascend to God by seeking God's presence and will. The opening and closing orations for the Ascension celebration of Eucharist speak to our own gradual ascension to the Father: "Make us joyful in the ascension of your Son Jesus Christ. May we follow him into the new creation, for his ascension is our glory and our hope.... Father, in this Eucharist we touch the divine life you give to the world. Help us to follow Christ with love to eternal life...." Clearly, the Church recognizes its mission to proclaim the Gospel, to baptize and to teach.

The shattering truth is that all this activity commanded by Christ at the time of his ascension is useless, if it is not motivated by a love which trusts uncompromisingly in God. Paul's letter to the Ephesians tells us that the Church is fullness on a universal scale—*pleroma*—because the Church is the presence of Christ in action. But *pleroma* is only full in love; Church is only Christian in love. Our participation in the Ascension Mystery can be a flutter of activity, but without love, that activity dissipates into a mere shadow of Gospel meaning.

The fact that the events surrounding the historical Christ occurred some twenty centuries ago makes poignant the reality that the Church's role is not just to wait out this eschatological tension by clutching to itself a small bundle of truths, but actively to prepare the way for the Second Coming of Christ by manifesting a living faith, open to the Spirit, which nurtures Christ's life in the world. Our awareness that Jesus Christ is still not with us in the fullness of his glory finds us hanging on that conditional phrase: "until he comes." The Ascension Mystery calls us to faith in the "Christ" of Jesus Christ. Do we suspect that Christian faith (or any religious belief, for that matter) is an elaborate hoax which perpetuates itself with illusory promises? If we come to view the Christ of our hearts as an opiate for our minds, then we should turn to prayer and the shared love of Christian fellowship to overcome our suspicions of unreality with a healthy dose of faith in action.

Do we fear that we have been abandoned by a God who is indifferent to our confusion and pain? If we begin to see the Resurrection as some superhuman, divine prerogative for escaping the human condition, then we must call ourselves back to the Incarnation Mystery, so that Jesus' humanity is not cynically divorced from Christ's divinity. We cannot call ourselves Christians if we keep hankering after a baby in a feeding trough. Those who cannot come to terms with a Risen and Glorified Christ who has promised to return at the end of time, should seriously ask themselves why they seem to prefer the baby of the Infancy Narratives to the Jesus who matured, challenged us all, and then ascended to be one with his Father.

The Ascension puts the pressure on all of us. We hear the promise of return at the end of time, but we have no way of determining when that may happen. We are given a promise of the Spirit to help us enliven our faith, but we soon discover that the Holy Spirit is not some power to be manipulated. God's Spirit is a presence to be recognized, respected, and heeded. God's transcendence is too removed to please us, yet God's immanence can be too close for our wavering hearts! We stand in the middle, feeling the pressure of faith's demands. Other than a few revealed truths about God who loves us and Jesus Christ who calls us toward that loving God's presence, we have no ultimate answers. Through our personal experience of God, we are called to live our faith hopefully. In our Gospel vision of a new creation inaugurated by Christ, we cherish our hope lovingly. With the presence of the Risen Christ experienced in the power of the Holy Spirit, we spend ourselves in love faithfully. Faith, hope, and love become the three angles of the spiritual triangle which defines the waiting Church.

With the solemnity of Pentecost, the Paschal Mystery culminates in the celebration of the loving presence of Christ now glorified. This loving presence of Christ in union with the Father is the Holy Spirit of God who founds the Church. John's Gospel account of the first appearance of the Risen Lord to his gathered disciples relates how Jesus came into the room, where they had locked themselves away from their fellow Jews. Jesus greeted the apostles with words of peace. After proving to them that he was, indeed, their friend and brother who had been crucified and raised from the dead, the Lord Jesus again spoke his greeting of peace. A greeting of peace was common among Jews of Jesus' day, and it continued to be the normative greeting for Christian believers during the early centuries of the Church. "Peace be with you," Jesus said (Jn. 20:21).

Earlier in the fourth Gospel we hear Christ tell the apostles:

> The Paraclete, the Holy Spirit
> whom the Father will send in my name,
> will instruct you in everything,
> and remind you of all that I told you.
> "Peace" is my farewell to you,
> my peace is my gift to you;
> I do not give it to you as the world gives peace (Jn. 14:26-27).

The gift of peace which Jesus brought to his fearful disciples was different from the ordinary greeting of peace among Jews. Jesus' gift of peace brought the Holy Spirit to a waiting world. The Greek word for Spirit used by the author—*pneuma*—means breath, or wind. "Then he breathed on them and said: 'Receive the Holy Spirit'" (Jn. 20:22). Christ breathed on them the Holy Spirit.

In one of the two Genesis creation accounts (cf. Gn. 1), the wind of God—*ruah*—sweeps over the waters of creation. In the other creation account (cf. Gn. 2), God creates humanity out of clay and blows the breath of life into the fashioned earth. After the Resurrection, Christ's breath on the apostles became the wind of a new creation, blowing new life into a redeemed humanity. This Spirit of God brought peace and the forgiveness of sins, gathered the disciples, and formed them into a people: the Body of Christ, the Church.

Luke's version of Pentecost (cf. Acts 2:1-11) describes the event which the Church has come to recognize as *the* Pentecost-event. All the apostles were filled with the Holy Spirit, depicted in terms of a rushing wind and tongues of flame. As in John's account, the presence of God's Spirit is marked by unity. The Holy Spirit brought together all the assembled into a unity which transcended linguistic boundaries. Paul later elaborated for the Christian churches an initial pneumatology which discussed the presence of the Holy Spirit in terms of the various spiritual gifts given to the Church for the upbuilding of faith and the proclamation of the Gospel. For instance, to the Corinthians Paul wrote: "There are different gifts but the same Spirit; there are different ministries but the same Lord; there are different works but the same God who accomplishes all of them in everyone. To each person the manifestation of the Spirit is given for the common good" (1 Cor. 12:4-7). The unity of the Spirit must be expressed in the unity of Christ's Church. If there is disunity, it is not the work of the Holy Spirit.

The Pentecost-event touches upon the pith of what we mean by "Church." The presence of the Holy Spirit in the celebration of the Church's sacraments is the fulfillment of Christ's promise to his disciples. When we call upon God to send the Holy Spirit upon the Eucharistic gifts (i.e., when the celebrant places his hands over these gifts of bread and wine in the prayer of epiclesis), we share in the presence of God's love. As Christians, we are called upon to live a Spirited existence. As an ecclesial body, we gather at the Eucharist to celebrate sacramentally the presence of the Christ-event. Without the presence of the Holy Spirit, the Eucharist would not be the sacrament of the Resurrection. Without this same Holy Spirit, Eucharist could not be a sign of unity in the Church. The Spirit is the pulse of our ecclesial life together. In eucharistic epiclesis, we call upon God to send us the Holy Spirit in order that the reality of the Christ-event may be actualized in us. How we recognize the power of the Holy Spirit among us determines, to some extent, how we live our relationship with God. Our understanding of the Spirit's workings among us will color our Christology, sacramentology, ecclesiology, eschatology, ecumenism, etc.

Through the power of the Holy Spirit, the mystery of Christ's salvific activity is made present because this Holy Spirit is the Spirit of the Risen Lord now glorified in God's presence. This is the Spirit of love, the unifying principle that binds believers into an ecclesial reality. Today's Holy Spirit is that same Spirit of Pentecost who filled the lives of early Christian believers with Christ's living presence. Our epicletic prayer asks God to keep sending the Holy Spirit, in order to continue the effects of that original Pentecost experience. Our prayer for the Spirit is a prolongation of Pentecost. As believers, we live a Spirited life in the new order; we are a new creation.

Because we live in God's Kingdom which is not fully realized, the gift of the Holy Spirit is an eschatological reality. Just as the Spirit enables us to stretch out our arms and pray "Abba," so also it is the Holy Spirit's guidance which moves us to open our hearts in a prayer of "Maranatha! Come, Lord." Our eucharistic assemblies become signs of the Messianic Banquet. Our gifts of bread and wine are permeated with the Holy Spirit, becoming spiritual food and drink—eschatological nourishment for life in God's Kingdom. Regardless of how oblivious to the Holy Spirit's work among us we can seem to be, participation in Church fellowship is a sharing in the life of that Spirit.

How we admire the religious experience of those gathered at that first Pentecost! What would we not give to experience that great rush of wind, those tongues of flame over our heads, and the phenomenon of glossolalia? Luke depicted this remarkable event in the history of humanity with the apocalyptic imagery current at the time of Jesus and during those early years of Church beginnings. Whatever occurred at Pentecost flowed from the apostles' experience of God in ineffable mystery. Whether what happened was more or less than depicted by scriptural accounts, one thing is certain: something quite momentous changed the course of human history. Here is the Church's christening. Here the Mystical Body of Christ leaves the sphere of potentiality and becomes actuality. Pentecost affected women and men to the core of existence, and effected that bonding of hearts and minds we call "Church."

The Mystical Body of Christ had been evolving from the dawn of human history. Pentecost was its baptism—a baptism in wind, fire, and spiritual gifts. The Eucharistic Prayer is a prayer of thanksgiving for the gift of Christ and the Church's baptism in the Spirit. The Holy Spirit's presence in the Church's history helps Christians to recognize Christ's living presence among them. The true Spirit of God enables us to live that Christ for others, forming us into the one Body of Christ rather than allowing us to remain a loosely knit federation of civil societies or humanitarian fraternities.

How we envy those fearful disciples behind their locked doors, as they witness the Risen Lord among them in an amazing way! What would we not give to see the Lord as *they* saw him, to hear his words of peace, and to feel his empowered breath upon us? Perhaps we would even be willing to exchange places with an embarrassed Thomas, to place our fingers on the Lord's wounds, if that would mean a strengthening of our faith. The miracle of Pentecost is that, in the power of the Holy Spirit, we *do* see, hear and feel Jesus Christ among us. If this is not so, then we are not opening ourselves to the Spirit's life. And if we are not living in the Holy Spirit, we have cut ourselves off from the Church, severed our relations with the Mystical Body, and denied our participation in the ever-evolving embrace of humanity in the arms of a patient and waiting God.

As our consciousness of Church grows, we realize more personally that the Holy Spirit is *our* Spirit; God's Spirit is for us. While the Risen Lord is in union with the Father, and we await the fullness of his presence in the Second Coming, the Holy Spirit enables us to experience the mystery of Jesus' living presence among us. We live in the age of the Spirit. Everything and everyone connected with this Spirit are linked to our relationship with God. In the Spirit of God, we become aware of the eternal life already enjoyed in Jesus' Name. We are only asked to believe in that Name, and the Holy Spirit helps us to believe.

Pentecost is a time for believing. Living in the Spirit of Pentecost puts our faith into action. The Holy Spirit is the great enabler, allowing what is possible in the realm of human potentiality to become actual in our activities of relating with the living God. The Spirit of God is our most significant benefactor who enriches us with the will to seek the presence and will of God, as well as the means to share that presence with others and to fulfill that will for others. The Spirit helps us to recognize the gifts we have and gives us the courage to share them with the faith-community. If we do not recognize our gifts, often enough the presence of the Holy Spirit will make them apparent to someone else. What a challenge it must be for leaders in today's Church to take seriously the task of discerning the spiritual gifts of others! But it is precisely just such a challenge which comes to the fore in contemporary ecclesial consciousness, both for the universal Church of Christ and every local Church within that greater whole. In a climate of rapid change, the Christian Church cannot afford to dodder around in anachronisms at the expense of authentic Gospel witness. This does not mean we should throw out the traditions, but that we should realize that what gifts exist in the fellowship of believers are meant to be exercised, shared, and used. This age of the Spirit may even surprise the institutional Church with the plethora of gifts it holds in store, waiting to be recognized and utilized in the furthering of Gospel witness.

The Holy Spirit also helps us all to recognize the gifts we are for one another. For this Spirit finds its way into the heart of the human person, no matter how sturdily that heart might have been hardened against discovery and penetration. God's Spirit descends to the depths of personality, where honesty rules the day. There, at the core of searching humanity, God breathes over our innermost being in ways as remarkable as those experienced in a locked room at Jerusalem or in a house echoing with an assortment of tongues. Challenging questions batter against the ramparts of our minds: Do we have the honesty to give that breath of God some room in our lives? Can we give the spiritual seed the opportunity to grow within the fragile environment of our human condition? Are we able to share our giftedness with others, even if such a sharing means exposure to rejection, ridicule, and misunderstanding? How do we recognize the giftedness of others, and what do we do with that recognition?

When we celebrate Pentecost on the turning wheel of becoming, we rejoice in the giftedness of humanity living in the Spirit. The Holy Spirit of God moves the human heart to be one with God and to nurture that oneness by becoming free enough to relate honestly with others. We are freed to grieve for ourselves and with others, without holding on to pain until it crystallizes into bitterness. We allow the Spirit room to teach us empathy and sympathy. The gifts of the Spirit build up the Church, fostering growth, progress, and revelation. The Holy Spirit strengthens what is weak, heals what is broken, and consoles what is experiencing unrest. God's Spirit frees the Body of Christ to live the faith it professes, and guides the Church on its pilgrim journey to the fullness of grace. But above all, the Spirit of God unifies us within ourselves and in our ecclesial relationships. For the Spirit's movement is an ecumenical one, prodding the Christian Churches with the extant scandal of disharmony and disunity. The Holy Spirit brings disparate parts into one and fuses them with love's flame.

During the centuries of the Church's evolution, many individuals and groups have arisen, claiming to have a corner on the market when it came to gifts of the Spirit. People have called attention to themselves, saying, "We have the Spirit in ways you do not know and cannot fathom. See what we can do; look at the tricks we can perform." When people claim to experience the Holy Spirit while they are cutting themselves off from other believing Christians, the Spirit of God is hardly at the source of the rupture. Anyone who asserts by word or action that the Holy Spirit can only work in certain ways or in specific places, at specified times, for certain individuals, is sorely mistaken. The Spirit cannot be contained, manipulated, or controlled. God's Spirit will move the hearts and minds of men and women in ways unique to those persons.

Inspiration is a communion with God's breath, giving life to those who seek God's presence. This breath flows freely and unpredictably. Perhaps we should turn the query "Where is the Holy Spirit?" toward ourselves: "Where are we?" When we live as if existence were some complex charade of posings, concealments, and timely impostures, then we will likely prefer to treat the idea of a Holy Spirit as some mechanical life-support system to be controlled at will rather than to relate with the living presence of the Holy Spirit as the very basis of our life together. The Church is essentially the life of this Holy Spirit.

Early Patristic writers often referred to any aspect of salvation's unfolding as *musterion*—mystery. The mystery of salvation history which emanated from God to humanity was revealed in the Holy Spirit and realized in the person of Jesus Christ. Christ became *the* mystery of God, the sacrament of divinity commingling with humanity. In a post-resurrectional framework, the Church gave and continues to give flesh and blood to Christ's presence in the world. As we participate in this ongoing sacrament of eternal life, God's Spirit continues to reveal further elaborations of that mystery to us. The Church is the mystery of our faith lived out in time. Our annual celebration of Pentecost invites us all to have faith in the mystery and to live that faith wholly in the power of the Spirit. The mystery of it all becomes a gradual yielding to life's inherent sacramentality.

VII
A Time for Living — ORDINARY TIME

In the psychology of color, green is often described in terms of hope, perseverance, even tenacity. There is a certain stick-to-it-iveness attached to the color green. Public relations people, advertising executives and commercial artists have shown statistically the hidden powers of color on the buying public. Different colors affect people differently. Some colors draw us toward them; others pull away from us. Psychologists who have researched the effects which the color spectrum can have on human behavior insist that color is a very important gauge for measuring human temperament. Some point out that a person's proclivity to choose one color over another, or to identify oneself with any particular color, will change over the years of varying life-rhythms. In other words, people will gravitate toward certain colors, depending on what deep-seated psychological factors are affecting their attempts to come to terms with, or to evade, various realities in their lives.

I can remember a time when I disliked the color green in most, if not all, its hues. Now I am drawn to green like a kitten to yarn! I have filled my room with a variety of potted plants and trees to counterbalance the effects of dried clumps of bittersweet, eucalyptus branches and prairie wildflowers I never seem to be without. My room has taken on new life, literally, and I think I understand at least part of what we mean when we say that green is the color of hope. This hope symbolized by the color green in the world of liturgical vestments has been alluded to enough during my lifetime that I consistently make the connotation whenever green is worn in a sacred assembly. Green is the color worn during that part of the Church Year known as Ordinary Time.

What is ordinary is usual, commonplace and regular, and there *is* something so ordinary about Ordinary Time. The Latin word from which "ordinary" is derived is *ordinarius*—according to order, regular, ordinary. When the Church Year reverts to Ordinary Time, it is reentering the major block of time marked out by the liturgical calendar's ordering of sacred time. This season of the liturgical year resonates with the lifetime aspects of becoming human and relating with the Holy. Ordinary Time unobtrusively centers on the long haul of Christian existence.

Most of us are very ordinary people who, for the majority of the time, lead quite ordinary lives. At least, we think of them as being ordinary. Even if each moment of existence is a physiological wonder of immeasurable complexity, it is an "ordinary" miracle we all share and take for granted most of the time. No matter how complex our lives can become, our fears and angers, raptures and rushes, aspirations and despondencies are normally experienced as part of the ordinary stuff of living on this planet; we consider them ordinary and mundane because everyone is dealing with life's needs, drives and desires. We have our hands full, just making it through each day: breathing, moving, eating, relating, working, praying, taking care of others. From the outside, the ordinary daily responsibilities of being a human person are anything but inconsequential.

But we consider repetitious life-rhythms as tedious and boring. We want to be entertained, excited and titillated. We may see our accustomed rhythms as wearisome ruts from which we must escape. We find the long haul unattractive. On the other hand, some of us tend to use the "ordinary" life as a refuge from personal involvement. A carefully confined life-style which does not allow any extraordinary events, other than absolutely inescapable ones to enter our orbit, can stifle our spirit and prevent us from becoming fully integrated human persons. Ordinary Time speaks to the matter of living out daily life. It is a season for all people, a season which presses home the poignant, if unremarkable, message that the Paschal Mystery is an event which each of us is to enter on a daily basis.

We find it easy to be thrilled with the "O" Antiphons of Advent, fascinated with the Incarnational light that Christmas sheds on our days. We can smear ashes on our foreheads and delve into Lenten asceticisms. We are eager to experience the sacred Triduum of Holy Week and to hear the trumpet tidings of Easter awe. We put ourselves in the places of Jesus' disciples as they experience God's Spirit in remarkable ways. But during Ordinary Time, we must center on the very ordinary rhythms of Christian commitment with its daily demands to die and rise in paschal awareness. Ordinary Time is a time for living. The green of this season's vestments connotes life, but it is also a color of hope, offering us all the grace to persevere with our own greening in the garden of a new creation.

If we are serious about Christianity, it should not take us long to realize that, regardless of how ordinary we might consider our lives to be, our Christian life together places very extraordinary demands upon those ordinary lives. At least, judging by how well we bring off the Gospel norms in our lives, we can assume these demands must be quite extraordinary. We have only to measure ourselves against the scale of the Beatitudes to see how well we are doing— how evangelical we are becoming—in our ordinary lives. Remember that Ordinary Time is a method by which we order our time into sacred time. And sacred time is both extraordinary and quite ordinary at the same time, depending on how we keep time with the Holy in our midst. To bring the time we spend in very ordinary ways on a day-today basis into God's presence, may take rather extraordinary effort on our part. Living the demands of Matthew 5 within the context of our everyday relations should be considered the most ordinary of ways to begin living the Gospel life, but how perplexing it can be to put spiritual theory into ethical practice.

How authentically poor in spirit can we become, if we insist on the illusion of self-sufficiency? When we experience no need for others, opting to rely solely on our own limited resources, it becomes arduous, if not impossible, to experience the radical need for God which we call spiritual poverty. We must learn to recognize our hunger for the presence of God and to experience our thirst for union with that living God. To live with the demands of this spiritual hunger and thirst entails suffering which can only be endured efficaciously by one who can live with purity of heart's soleness of purpose. "All for the greater honor and glory of God" runs the pious axiom. The one who lives this axiom can be said to be pure of heart because such an aspiration requires single-heartedness. If we are to be blessed with purity of heart, we must realize that an elaboration of the beatitudinal approach to our everyday human relations asks of us nothing less than being patient, gentle, compassionate and merciful in all our relationships. If we are unable to mourn for ourselves and to share the grief of another in empathy, then we are far from living the ordinary Gospel life. Unless we are willing to live peacefully, to promote peace among all peoples, and to make peace in the nitty-gritty arena of interpersonal relationships, we make the basic Christian principles we profess seem extraordinarily elusive.

There has been, and continues to be, a strong current of Christian spirituality which centers on the imitation of Christ in his mysteries as a practical means for embracing the Gospel. All of us should model our lives on Jesus Christ, but we will articulate the particulars of such modelings in unique ways, depending upon our personalities and the presence of grace. Instead of physically carrying crosses through our streets in order to imitate Christ in his passion (as would, for instance, still extant groups of *flagellantes* who tote crosses and scourge themselves for ostensibly penitential reasons), we will enter the paschal dimensions of Christ's suffering and death within our own lives in unique expressions of lived faith.

The Eucharistic New Testament readings for Ordinary Time offer us the whole Gospel gamut of Christ's life and teaching. We are faced with the Christ who heals what is broken and hurting in his presence. We hear the Christ who teaches in a radical fashion, always adhering to the truth. We cannot miss Christ preaching words of encouragement, hope and promise. There is the praying Christ who wanders off to lonely desert locales in order to be alone with his Father. Often we are reminded of the celebrating Christ who seems to love parties, attending banquets and sitting in table fellowship with social and religious outcasts of his day. (I am always amazed when I hear someone say that Jesus never smiled or laughed. For a man who did not smile, he certainly attended his share of parties! He even described the Kingdom of God in terms of a grand party.) The Gospels also show us a Christ who is forever sharing his time and energy with those in need. We find a patient and listening Christ who consistently hammers his Gospel message into the thick Galilean skulls of his disciples. But above all, we always discover that loving Christ who can be at home with anyone open to the experience.

If we are going to imitate the extraordinary Christ in our ordinary ways, we too have to heal, teach, preach, and pray to the best of our abilities. We must learn to celebrate life, to share it with others, and to love the living of it. Ordinary Time is the time for all of this, and more. But there is a catch. A few qualifiers condition our responses to the demands of Gospel living. And it seems to me that these conditioners are absolutes: universality, commonality, eucharisticality and sacramentality. Gospel integrity insists that our Christian witness be universal in scope. Gospel integration unites us in the fellowship of shared life and love. Gospel integrality urges us to be bread for one another during our ordinary days of sharing the one bread of Christ. Gospel efficacy forces us to live the mystery of it all for one another in extraordinary ways. Come to think of it, one could make a case for these four Gospel absolutes representing the traditional four marks of Church: universality (catholic), commonality (apostolic), eucharisticality (one), sacramentality (holy). Does not the meat of Ordinary Time appear to be extraordinary fare after all?

From the Egyptian desert tradition of the Christian monastic solitaries, come to us these two episodes translated by Sister Benedicta Ward, S.L.G., in her book entitled *The Sayings of the Desert Fathers* (London: Mowbrays, 1975):

> Abba Lot went to see Abba Joseph and said to him, "Abba, as far as I can, I say my little office, I fast a little, I pray and meditate, I live in peace and, as far as I can, I purify my thoughts. What else can I do?" Then the old man stood up and stretched his hands towards heaven. His fingers became like ten lamps of fire and he said to him, "If you will, you can become all flame" (p. 88).

> A brother came to the cell of Abba Arsenius at Scetis. Waiting outside the door he saw the old man entirely like a flame. (The brother was worthy of this sight.) When he knocked, the old man came out and saw the brother marvelling. He said to him, "Have you been knocking long? Did you see anything here?" The other answered, "No." So then he talked with him and sent him away (p. 11).

Are we called to "become all flame" in our experience of God? We may not find ourselves glowing like burning embers, but we should manifest a certain Christian light to those we encounter during the ordinary flow of our lives.

The Risen Christ should shine through us, if our Christian commitment is more than merely nominal affiliation. But talk of light, flame, and shining in the Lord smacks of mysticism, from which most of us shy. We assume that mystical prayer and experience are supernatural phenomena reserved for an elite group of extraordinary and highly gifted individuals. Unfortunately, I think we too easily overlook the possibility of promoting an ordinary mysticism for all Christian believers who take their faith seriously. Why can we not all be Christian mystics? Is there a practical mysticism for the ordinary Christian— one which does not dilute the essential meaning of mysticism, while allowing room for the real call to divinization that we hear in the Gospel's proclamation?

The statement that all Christians are called to be mystics should be articulated in terms general enough to encompass the unification and communion to which all are called in the process of surrendering to God's will, without narrowing the scope by adding too much accumulated mystique of elitist Christianity. All Christians are "Christian" to the extent that they are part of Christ's Body. The Christian mystic exists within the Church. The mystic participates in the mystery of the Church—active participation in divine life. Christian mysticism is authentic only to the extent that it is ecclesial. In the life of the Church, the mystic lives Christian love which unites the person with Christ, as well as with other Christians. We are all called to this kind of love, this active participation in divine life. Each of us is called to union and communion in the order of grace, which is the very nature of ecclesial reality. Mystical experience can be seen as that ordinary, graced union to which all Christians are called. Mysticism is the unified oneness of will and harmonized communion of love between a person and the source of meaning—experienced as most real, most vital, simple, whole and, ultimately, ineffable.

Teresa of Avila likened this union to the joining of two lighted candles so that their wicks, wax, and light all become one. Both Henry Suso and John Tauler described the nature of this union as a drop of water lost in a cask of wine. It is an overwhelming experience of oneness. An interior unification of personality occurs—melding what is disparate and conflicting with silence, tranquillity, and unity. Here is the "still point" mentioned by poets and mystics. This oneness is God and, as so many holy men and women have put it, mystical experience is to be "one with the One." Johannes Meister Eckhart proposed that the human person always try to live an "evenness" in all aspects of life, if he or she really hopes to join human will to divine will. The process of divinization requires this kind of moderation and tempering if we are to embrace God's will within us and truly become one with the One. This is the harmony of conflicts which expresses itself fully in a harmony of silence. Here are the rest and peace which flow in the silent whisper of embrace. Christian love, to which we all are called, harmonizes the various aspects of life so that a oneness of wills between God and the human person can occur. Selfless love is the mark of this communion—a passage from self to other, from egocentricity to allo-centricity.

Mystical union embraces reality. The mystic discovers the moment of the Eternal, the divine present in the here-and-now. John Tauler said that all is real when the past and the future have dissolved into the now. The mystic embraces the present in God's presence. In grace, we Christian believers experience what is most real. We also experience what is most vital in existence: love. We find the gift of true self, lived in the ethical demands of charity. To be a lover is to live what is most vital. We can live the Gospel vision more simply and single-heartedly if we but love. The mystic experiences wholeness in the One and oneness in the whole of his or her being.

Pierre Teilhard de Chardin wrote of a unification in love by which the entire universe is in the process of convergence: communion with God is happening through the universal transformation of matter in Christ. Teilhard de Chardin was a remarkable man who experienced an amazing relationship with God, a relationship he expressed through his scientific and philosophical writings. But for most of us, it is difficult to attempt any articulation of the experience of God. Ultimately, most mystics who have taken pen in hand have been forced to admit its ineffability. Mystical union approaches the "inexpressible abyss," "rich nothing," "sacred wilderness," "bare pure ground," "nameless," and "formless." We are humbled by the impoverishment of our language to express our experience of God.

The mystic's witness is that all are called to union with God whose grace is meant for all. We must live the Gospel authentically and be open to God's love and workings. The Christian mystic embraces Gospel life for the sake of others. In our ordinary lives, we may not stand luminously in our homes or walk our streets with fingers aflame, but we are called to experience union with God in the most ordinary ways. Ordinary Time reminds us that the Christian duty of carrying Easter light into a waiting world is here for the duration. The Transfiguration feast occurs relatively midway through the season of Ordinary Time. Christ in the Mystery of Transfiguration calls us all to shine in the effulgence of loving union with God. If we do so, we are the mystics—quite ordinary mystics—caught up in an extraordinary gift of dawn's breaking.

> Blaze of dazzling white
> on the mount in light
> suspends the mind's eye
> with mingled awe and fright.
>
> What is this icon bright
> but the sacred given sight?

> This flesh encountered, why,
> if not to soften our plight?
>
> Eons call us to that height
> to irradiate, glow, and quite
> to be scintillant against the lie
> that the icon is of the night.

It would be awesome to discover that Teilhard de Chardin's vision of the physical universe's convergence upon God is actually taking place in the routine energy and movement of the cosmos. To think that the universe is actually converging upon the simple presence of love pulsating at its core, permanently places our "ordinary" time in the perspective of sacred time. Teilhard de Chardin used the image of the "cone of time," spiralling toward the Omega-point of Christ in his fullness, to express the vast movement of spiritual becoming which he sensed around him. He saw the universe as an ocean "stirred by the Spirit," as it slowly *becomes* Christ in his fullness.

Teilhard de Chardin called for a common, universal mysticism in which unity might be achieved by means of the convergence of the many into the One. This mysticism would view the universe as a whole, coming together. Unity would be achieved over the stretch of time through convergence upon a personal God, not by identification with an impersonal God within the common ground. All reality would be transformed, not escaped, through religious consciousness; transcendence would be attained by human effort, not by release from effort. He envisioned unity as possible only in fullness, not in emptiness, because God fills the world with a presence which gives each element an intrinsic value of its own. Chardin's universal mysticism would cut a path between the road to communion with God and that to communion with earth: it would focus on communion with God *through* earth. He saw a universal and transforming love as the dynamic within his world mysticism because, in love, everything and everyone becomes sacred.

This vision of a converging cosmos in universal love is an awesome horizon seen through the poetic eye of a scientist and seer. Whether or not we find his universal mysticism to be feasible or realistic, aspects of Teilhardian spirituality resonate with the ordinary mysticism to which all Christians are called. What truer meaning for the Church's existence could be found than our ordinary, day-to-day efforts at bringing Christ to fullness? And how better to approach the birth of love's fullness at time's end than to concentrate on bringing ourselves to fullness through the vitalization of Gospel principles? Our fullness will be found in our exigency to become human persons. Throughout the liturgical year we meet epiphanies of Jesus Christ which present us with deeper revelations of how to go about the task of becoming a person. But we will miss the simple truth within the various mysteries of Christ, if we overlook the omnipresent power of love in those mysteries.

Teihard de Chardin was right. There *is* a presence of love pulsating at the center of all. There *must* be, in order to give any coherence to what the human soul is about in its search for personal meaning and universal value. We strive to touch that simple core of being with our lives—our very ordinary lives. The miracle we celebrate repeatedly during our liturgical celebrations of Ordinary Time is the religious intuition that all is lovable in Christ. By virtue of our Gospel commitment, if not by our own graced experience, we know that we are to love with a universal love because the fullness of love in the Glorified Christ is a love which knows no boundaries, walls, limitations, conditions, or qualifications. Our immediate problem is loving as Jesus Christ loved, for it is in Christ (and *as* Christ) that we are to love. But even if we spend our lives learning the meaning of Christ's love (and surely we need to spend them in this labor of love), our conscious endeavors to do so move with that pulse of universal love at the center of it all!

Before the Church Year resumes its annual turning with a return to the Advent season, the long season of Ordinary Time winds to a close with the celebration of Christ the King. This solemnity seems a most appropriate way to end, thematically, one liturgical year, as well as to set the tone for the Advent season of the following year. Having passed through the mysteries of Christ in the liturgical celebrations of a year—from birth and ministry to passion, death, resurrection, and ascension—we now celebrate the Universal and Cosmic Christ, Christ the King and Firstborn of Creation, Christ Glorified and in union with the Father, and Christ ready to return in glory at the end of time. The Cosmic Christ whom we celebrate on this day witnesses to truth, the eternal reality of God's love. By witnessing to the love of truth and the truth of love, Christ exercises kingship. As the Kingdom of God among us, Jesus Christ is the Living Word, the Word of life and truth. In union with the Father's will, Jesus *is* truth.

Christ the King is a feast for poets, mystics, liturgists, and musicians. It accords us the opportunity to try to express liturgically what we sense of the tremendous mystery shared with us in the person of Jesus Christ. In the name of this Christ, our life in Church fellowship and mutual service happens "so that God may be all in all" (1 Cor. 15:28). At the end of Ordinary Time we pray that we might share in Christ's Kingship. Our sharing is based on service; our serving is expressed in sharing. The scope of our Christian witness is universal because what is universal embraces what is personal in the loving presence of Christ. Now is the time for living and, always, an occasion for loving. Our ordinary task is to make evident, by whatever means possible, God's extraordinary presence. We can attain this objective by living transparently in God's grace. Our lives will be transfigured before the world when our love becomes diaphanous, allowing resurrectional light to reveal our hearts with a translucency born of simplicity. The art of living simply converts the ordinariness of our days into the extraordinary awarenes of who we are in God's presence: pure gift—and that, for each other.

VIII
The Inspirable Life

We find ourselves back at the beginning. The circle has no end. The circle is a rainbow reflected in life's redemptive pool, gathering the entire spectrum of colors in its gentle sweep around all our realities. We stand in this pool and feel the movement of these rainbows joined end to end, filling in the circle of covenant, renewal, and promise. The circle rounds out our perspectives. It calls us into its center, in whose depths we gradually come to know identity, meaning, and wholeness as we follow the circle's rhythms again and again. For in the whirling, circling, concentrating movement, we allow ourselves the freedom and facility of repetition. In the circle of the Church's liturgical year, we revisit the salvation events which our memories hold sacred, but we also reenter the mystery of Christ in those events, thereby renewing our year, the season, every day, and each moment in the grace of that shared mystery. We recognize ourselves in each season's spiritual signs. Depending on how fully we enter the mystery of the season, we come to accept Christ's presence as the potential fullness of our own human becoming.

The mysteries we celebrate during the Church Year are all invitations to God's Kingdom. Each presents us with the possibility of communion—not just the idea of some future union with God in heaven, but the real experience of communion with God through the gift of eternal life already made present in the Risen Christ. In Advent, we watch and wait for the Word. We know ourselves as dependent, vigilant, and receptive. During the Christmas season, we give birth to that Word spoken in the depths of our hearts. We know ourselves as incarnational, evangelical, and active. Lent finds us giving and forgiving. We know ourselves as incomplete, needy, and only too human. Holy Week draws us into the Paschal Mystery of humanity's salvation. We know ourselves as stripped, emptied, and always in the process of dying. The Easter Mystery celebrates the miracle of resurrection. We know ourselves as renewed, fulfilled, and ever in the grace of rising. During Pentecost, we celebrate our roots in the reality of Church. We know ourselves as Spirited, gifted, and part of one Body. And in Ordinary Time, we experience the extraordinary demands of Gospel life. We know ourselves as transformed, transfigured, and ineluctably challenged.

The round of liturgical seasons is, indeed, a wheel of becoming. The wheel invites us to become who we are meant to be in God's presence. The Church Year moves us to enter that presence, repeatedly and consciously. If we are aware of the Church's sacramentality, we will discover ourselves in those mysteries we celebrate so solemnly. The cycle of liturgical seasons is quite simply an aid for us to focus our minds and center our hearts on the vivifying presence of Christ among us. The Church Year helps us to enter sacred time and to incorporate its timeless time in our own personal histories and times. Through its forms, colors, sounds, tastes, smells, and touches, the world of liturgy invites us to enter sacred space and to stand in a placeless space without any boundaries or limitations. Though we presently define ourselves by our physiological coordinates on a space-time continuum, our definition of "reality" pales before the spiritual intimations of reality beyond the empirical veil. We are each a wheel of becoming within the liturgical wheel of becoming. We are wheels within wheels. We compenetrate one another's mysteries, as we participate in eternal life. The world is continually being regenerated by the grace of divinization. Though it may be a slow-moving one, our circling is a spiral of convergence—encircling a New Jerusalem to be born.

Our surest wisdom will be found in allowing ourselves to be guided by God's Spirit. We want to live in a spiritually animated way. We hope to be inspired. But what does that really mean? When we say someone is inspired, often we concern ourselves with something that person has created. Artistic inspiration is a common notion. When we read great works of literature, appreciating the mesh of ideas, images, and feelings created by a writer's skillful work with words, we refer to his or her creative inspiration. When we listen to the textures, tonalities, rhythms and musical ideas woven into a whole by the musician's artful euphony in the medium of sound, we are awed by the genius of musical composition. We chalk it up to musical inspiration. We see and touch artifacts created by talented people who blend movement, form, texture, and color into inspiring works of art: sculpture, ceramics, pottery, painting, weaving. We equate the process of creating with inspiration and, of course, this equation touches upon a truth. Those who involve themselves with artistic creativity do find themselves resonating with cosmic rhythms, asking metaphysical questions, and attempting to make universal statements through whatever media they might be employing in artistic expression. At times, they may find themselves working feverishly under the creative impulse of inspiration, though it is likely that the majority of time spent in creative output is the result of pure hard labor.

But there is also something to say about becoming what is created, over and above merely being the creator. If the inspiration with which we concern ourselves in our paschal awareness of participation in Christ's life, death and resurrection is breathing in God's life and love, then we would do well to breathe. We may be poets, in many senses, but until we become the poem, we do not fully take shape in creation's living waters stirred by God's breath.

And that breath is the presence of the Word giving us life. We become the music, if we dare to follow the rhythms of divine life. We are the dance and the Spirit is the dancer. The more we enter the mystery of Christ, the more inspired is the dance. We are the words, the sounds, forms, and colors. We are the loom, the silken strands, the design, the tapestry: we are all, if we are living in the Spirit.

Our music, dance, and design center on creative force. We converge on the Word, born in silence. If we live in the Spirit—if we are inspirable—we chant the poetry of life, invoking God to help us allow what *is* truly to be. We become Love's artifact, the sounding board for that silent Word in the world. By entering the mysteries of Christ, again and again, we experience personal regeneration. Through our wholeness we help to form a Spirited creation; by our holiness we celebrate that creation in the Spirit. This is life as it is meant to be lived. This is inspirable life, a share in eternity's promise. The liturgical year is a wheel of becoming which invites us to be one with the Word and inspires us to become part of a renewed creation —moving in a convergent circle of love.